DIVORCE BUCKET LIST

One Woman's Powerful Journey of Self-Discovery and Healing Through Divorce and How You Can Heal Too

JENNIFER HARRIS

© Jennifer Harris 2021

Published in the United States by Jennifer Harris

First Edition, 2021

ISBN: 978-1-7379649-0-2

All rights reserved. No part of this publication may be reproduced, distributed, or transmitted in any form or by any means, including photocopying, recording, or other electronic or mechanical methods, without the prior written permission of the publisher, except in the case of brief quotations embodied in critical reviews and certain other noncommercial uses permitted by copyright law. For permission requests, contact Jennifer Harris at hello@divideguide.com.

This is a work of creative nonfiction. The events are portrayed to the best of the author's memory. While all the stories in this book are true, some names and identifying details have been changed to protect the privacy of the people involved. The conversations in the book all come from the author's recollections, though they are not written to represent word-for-word transcripts. Rather, the author has retold them in a way that evokes the feeling and meaning of what was said, and in all instances, the essence of the dialogue is accurate. The reader should not consider this book anything other than a work of literature.

Although this publication is designed to provide accurate information regarding the subject matter covered, the publisher and the author assume no responsibility for errors, inaccuracies, omissions, or any other inconsistencies herein. This publication is meant as a source of valuable information for the reader, however, it is not meant as a replacement for direct expert assistance. If such level of assistance is required, the services of a competent professional should be sought.

To everyone who believed in me, I love you!

To everyone reading, I believe in you!

Table of Contents

The End 1
   "I Want A Divorce" 3
   The Fears 6
   Your Turn—Overcome Fear 10
Playing Basketball 17
   How to Enjoy Being Alone 23
The Bucket List 25
   The Attack 27
   The Weight 32
   The Contract 38
   The List 42
   Creating Your Divorce Bucket List 46
Must-Do Mama 49
   Tips for Developing a Must-Do Mindset 57
Here I Go Again, On My Own 59
   Minus One 59
   Plus Zero 70
   Date Yourself Challenge 73
Learning To Share 75
   Sharing The Blues 75

Sharing The Burdens And Bliss	77
My Co-Parenting Tips	78
It's A Marathon	81
Race Running Hacks	89
Progress, Not Perfection (Yet)	91
Old, New, Borrowed, Blue	103
Something Old	103
Something New	107
Something Borrowed	113
Something Blue	120
Exploration	127
Doing The Things	141
Empowering Activities	141
Visualization For Healing	144
Healing Through Regimen	149
The Crown	153
Notes	171
Acknowledgments	173
Work With Jenn	177
About The Author	179

THE END

It was the darkest point of the night. My parents had thrown one of their infamous summer pool parties, and everyone had already headed home. After their typical post-party cleaning, my parents had gone inside to get ready for bed.

Me? I submerged myself in the pool. I closed my eyes as I felt the water consume me and decided that I would hold my breath until I slipped away from all of the things I could no longer bear. I started to feel a slight lack of oxygen but remained determined in my escape. I opened my eyes and saw blurry stars in the sky through the water before closing them again, making the pool wetter with my tears. "It's okay; it'll be over soon, no more suffering," I told myself as I started to struggle with the lack of oxygen.

As I started to fight my panic, I heard my mother screaming my name. I opened my eyes to the sound as the light began to pour back into my vision. Something about the shrill way she was screaming woke me from the mistake I was about to make. Before that night, there had never been a single point in my life that I even considered ending it. However, at this point, I had hit rock bottom. I was eight years into a toxic marriage. I had been behaving in a way I was ashamed of because I had not confronted past traumas or all the heavy things that had occurred in the relationship. Fueled by copious amounts of alcohol during the party, I had reached the end of my ability to deal with the toxicity that was happening in my marriage.

After years of enduring a chaotic atmosphere, I just couldn't take it anymore. Because of what I now know are my ingrained abandonment issues, I was unable to walk away from my marriage. Instead, I almost walked away from my own life. Two months later, my husband finally pulled the plug and decided he wanted a divorce. Only two years, almost to the day, after the night I nearly ended everything, I found myself standing on a stage in London, in front of thousands of people. I shared my story, empowering them to push through hard times, teaching them what I had learned, and finally putting my crown back on my head as I fell back in love with myself and my life.

After hitting that rock bottom, I finally decided that things needed to change. Even though I wasn't the one to walk away from the marriage, I am forever grateful that I got the coaching, counseling, and tools that I needed to flip everything around completely. I ended up accidentally creating a process to heal using all the things I had been learning. The business coaching that I had been practicing evolved into my personal life. I was able to completely turn everything around and go from lacking the ability to cope, being terrified, frozen, and stuck, to completely living the life I desired. I found myself again. I loved myself again. I was able to rebuild. If it weren't for the things I learned along the way, I never would have found myself on that stage helping others, let alone where I am now: thriving.

This is my story. I hope it helps you find your way to full recovery through and after your divorce. I hope this story enables you to rebuild. I hope this book gives you tools to reach your desired outcomes through and after your divorce and that you never find yourself as desperate, afraid, alone, and hopeless as I was during that moment in the pool.

I'm now excited to get out of bed each day. I'm living life with a purpose that I had previously only dreamed of doing. I live with gratitude. And, even though I don't have everything I want yet, I know that I'm on my way to achieving all of my dreams and desires. This is my story and how I used an accidentally created process, my Divorce Bucket List, to go from no longer being able to bear reality to ultimately thriving and loving myself and life again.

"I WANT A DIVORCE"

While standing in our beautiful gowns (or suits)—which we probably paid way too much for—at the altar of our dream weddings, saying our vows and making our commitments, we never imagine the possibility of those four nasty words. The furthest thing from our minds in that moment is: Will we be able to face the ongoing struggles of daily life in the years to come? No, we are living in a beautiful, hopeful, and happy moment.

Unfortunately, many of us come to realize that, for whatever reason, the marriage is broken, and we end up hearing or having to gain the courage to say these four life-altering words:

I want a divorce.

I'll never forget the moment my ex-husband said those words to me. I had confronted him in another ugly fight, which had steadily become our norm of communication in the unhealthy world we built our relationship around. After both of us had spent years hurting each other, putting each other through our biggest relationship fears and struggles, he had finally reached his breaking point.

I grew up believing marriage was permanent, that there was no such thing as divorce. So, hearing these words, and worse, accepting them, was the hardest thing I've ever done—and I've pushed out two healthy baby boys! But there I was, my now ex-husband putting his head in his hands, sighing heavily, and repeating, "Jenn, I want a divorce." I had no clue that I was about to embark on the scariest, most difficult, but also the most enlightening journey of my life. Even though I had been at the end of my rope in the marriage for years, I was terrified by this actual decision!

Since going through my divorce, I have learned that sometimes the best things in life come after walking away from things we thought were forever ours. While something might be the best thing for us, it does not mean that it is easy. It's never easy to do something that will involve an entire process of discomfort, mainly because the fear in our minds holds a powerful force over our decisions.

That September, when I was done with my six-hour crying session in the fetal position on the bathroom floor—I should say sobbing uncontrollably, to the point where my entire t-shirt was soaked in tears, reality hit me. *I'm getting a divorce!* I had set my entire life goals, dreams, and visions around the family that we had already created—my husband, me, and our two little boys. I had not even thought to envision a life that separated that family or caused my children to live in a broken home. But now, as I stared at my swollen face in the mirror, I realized I had to accept this harsh reality. My marriage had to end, and maybe, just maybe, it could be for the better.

I decided to write this book about my divorce journey from suffering to recovery to help others get through what I went through and share some things I learned along the way. These lessons assisted me in the grief process associated with this type of life-altering change. I will share stories that will make you laugh, ones that will make you cry, and some that will probably hit close to home if you are going through your own divorce. Most importantly, I am going to share practical exercises throughout this book that will help you begin your healing journey to rediscovering yourself and falling in love with life again.

As I begin writing this, I am sitting on the beach two years after those dreaded words were spoken. Moments before I started writing, I was washed over with a sense of peace that didn't seem possible months ago.

Thankfully, I had already been on a journey of self-development before the divorce happened, but if that's not you, it's not too late to start!

I am so honored to be with you through this journey and need you to know that you are not alone.

The Fears

It doesn't matter if you have been on the receiving end of those dreadful words or if you had to be the one to summon the courage to say them. Either way, I can guarantee you that your brain felt weighed down by the unknown shortly after the decision was made. There were so many questions that went through my brain within such a short period of time that there were days I didn't even know if I took a breath or remembered to eat. All I could do at first was focus on the "what now?" questions running through my mind.

I want to share some of the biggest worries I struggled with at the beginning of my divorce and show you how they played out in the end. But first, I want to explain why you have to stop overthinking right now. Instead, you need to take the time and energy you are spending on worrying and refocus it toward coming up with an action plan and taking baby steps toward your new future. After all, your new future could be one of the most exciting chapters of your life. Still, you will never make it there if you do not start taking some action, taking control over the fear in your mind—controlling your every movement—and begin the growing process.

It took me some time, but I learned how to control my thoughts and view the things that were happening around me more positively—notice I didn't say happening *TO* me. I started to see the light at the end of the tunnel. I also started to appreciate the steps in my journey towards the other side of divorce.

Here are some of the thoughts that went through my mind at the beginning—and what ended up actually happening:

* *"I will never be able to survive as a single household income."*

One year before we decided to get a divorce, my husband and I decided that I would leave my well-paying job as a financial software business analyst to follow my dream of being self-employed. I was still bringing in some income but was in business-building mode, so I incurred considerable business expenses. I had only been living my dream career for one year when the divorce began, and I was terrified I would have to go back to a corporate job and sacrifice my dreams. None of my fears came true; I found ways to adapt and learned that money is quite literally a renewable resource. I was able to find new ways to bring in money, fight for the money I deserved from the marriage, and apply some creative budgeting. Little did I know that going through this divorce would also create a whole new dream for me. In the end, I was able to remain self-employed. Not only that, but I was able to start a second business, write a book, and discover my dream of one day creating a retreat for people going through a divorce and help them begin their journey of rediscovering themselves. At the time of publication, this dream is in the works!

* *"I am failing my children by splitting the family up."* *

When we started the divorce, my boys were five and nine. All they had ever known was the family home we had. I was so worried that I ruined their lives and failed them because I could no longer provide that stable, complete family for them. I would think things like: If only I had been a better wife and done this or that better, then my children's lives wouldn't be ruined. I felt like a complete failure because, as a mother, spending any time away from your children just does not seem natural. While our home possessed many memories that included a full family unit, it was also broken. My ex-husband and I got married quickly and at a very young age, and I truly believe that neither of us was ready for the type of commitment that marriage requires. We both had our own personal growth to do and our own inner demons to battle before we could honestly give ourselves to someone else in a healthy way. Because of that, our marriage suffered greatly - ultimately, so did our children. Now that I can look back with clarity and perspective, separating was the best possible thing we could do for our children. Both homes are now places of peace instead of war. And, even though we all had to adjust, I think giving children a sense of peace is far more important than feeling like you did it right or wrong by someone else's book. My children have never been happier! Sure, they had to cope just like we did, but when you give them healthy outlets to process everything, two homes really can be a better thing for them.

* *"The court process and lawyer fees are going to ruin me."* *

I was terrified because everyone told me about the horrible financial impact a divorce would have on me. I don't have to say too much here other than that I figured everything out, and you can too. I found ways, and you will find them too. It's so cliché, but things truly do find a way of working out. Shopping around for lawyers helped me to get a quality one at a reasonable rate. Creating a budget also helped me find counsel I could afford, more on those topics later. I was also terrified of the asset split, but once

I got organized and created an action plan, I could go to bat for myself—with the help of legal counsel—and get what I deserved. I know several people who have even found success representing themselves instead of hiring counsel. Just take deep breaths on this one, and trust that it will work out—take it one step at a time.

* *"I will never find another partner because I'm damaged goods."* *

Wow, can you believe I actually told myself this for over a year!? I mean, I was now a thirty-two-year-old single mom. I have a lot of guy friends, and not once in our recent years of chit-chat have I heard any of them say anything like, "I just wish I could find a divorced, single mom to fall in love with." Divorce is mental wreckage; it tears you down and makes you feel like you are an unworthy failure. I had several terrible fake-lationships, as I call them, after my divorce. They didn't fail because I wasn't worthy. They failed because I had neglected to take the time to fall back in love with myself first. My Divorce Bucket List helped me rediscover myself, find joy and passion in life, and love myself again. It wasn't until after engaging in my Divorce Bucket List journey that I ended up meeting an absolutely amazing man. I am now, as I write this, in the healthiest relationship I've ever been in. I found this relationship because I found myself, I love myself, and I now believe that I am worthy.

Your Turn—Overcome Fear

The other night, I had a pretty weird dream, and it reminded me of how much fear can paralyze us. In my dream, I was in some type of creative speech class. I don't know if that type of class exists, but it was a public speaking class where you had to come up with speeches on the fly. Random dream details: we were in this big banquet hall, and everyone brought dishes to share, but they were basic dishes like veggie trays. In my dream, I was given the task of coming up with a speech on demand. The speech had to last at least ten minutes and be about the food that was brought into the class.

The food concept was strange, but even stranger was the fact that I was utterly terrified. I love public speaking in real life, but I was scared in my dream because I couldn't figure out what to say about the ridiculous topic. What was I supposed to say for ten minutes about bland food? "Oh, look at this carrot." "This veggie tray looks delicious." I was so panicked as other people in the class took their turns, knowing that it was almost my turn, and I had no idea what to say.

Suddenly, my dream fast-forwarded—like they tend to do—to me sitting on a platform so high above the ground that I could not jump down. There was no way to get off this platform. Literally, no way; there was no elevator or anybody there to help me. I could still see the class from a distance, but my fear paralyzed me and took over. The reality of how high up I was set in. I didn't think to do anything rational like yell at the audience for help. I also didn't think to look around and assess my surroundings.

After some time, I realized that I was irrationally afraid before I figured out whether or not there was something to be fearful of. Once I calmed down, I was able to assess the entire situation. I looked around and noticed there was a pole-like apparatus near me. I also realized there were a bunch of people within yelling distance. So, I took a deep breath in my dream and shouted to the class, asking them to get a fire truck with a ladder to help me down.

The class ran over and helped me. As my fear started to subside from realizing that help was on the way, I realized I could actually assist myself. As it turned out, I hadn't even needed to call for help because, after further examination of the situation, I could easily slide down to the ground using the nearby pole.

My crazy dream resembles our reality in a lot of ways. Things happen in life, and we find ourselves in situations where we become paralyzed by fear—fear of the unknown, of things we are afraid could happen to us, of judgment and failure. Just like in my dream, it's up to us, and *only* us, to overcome that fear. And it's important to overcome that fear before it clouds our judgment so much that we can't find ourselves again. In my divorce, especially in the beginning, there were so many times where I was frozen in fear. It wasn't until I started taking action with the things that I'll be sharing in this book that I could finally assess my situation, begin to rebuild, and find peace.

Have you ever had one of those life-defining moments? You know, the ones where something happens, and you get goosebumps everywhere because you know that what you just heard or learned will forever have an impact on your life. That happened to me a few years ago while attending a business conference in Las Vegas.

My come-to "I can do this, even if it will be hard" moment came as I was sitting in a convention hall surrounded by thousands of others within my industry. We had just undergone three days of intense training for our minds, skills, and business knowledge. In the end, the host got up on stage, dimmed the lights, and started talking to us about how we were probably ready to take all of the training we received and make changes in our lives using that new knowledge. He went on to explain that we needed to be prepared because whenever you change something significant in your life—whether it's something you're purposefully changing or not—the universe is going to fight back to try to hold you where you are.

Before I continue my story, I don't want you to think that I'm some crazy person when I talk about the universe. As the nerdy person I am, I'm mostly speaking scientifically regarding energy transfer when referring to anything regarding the universe. It makes sense if you think about it; there is a transfer of energy all the time. Suppose a car runs into a tree: energy transfers. You give someone a high-five: energy transfers. Have you ever been in the best mood and then encountered someone acting miserable and noticed your mood level drop after the encounter? Yup, that was the result of energy transfer!

As we go about living our lives, we encounter many different methods and levels of energy transfer.

This speaker referred to the science of energy transfer; if we are operating at a certain level of energy, everything—and everyone

—around us is used to interacting with us at that level. If you decide you're going to make a significant change, which means you are changing your current energy level, you will get resistance because it's not what those around you are used to.

Now that we have that explanation covered, back to the story... The speaker dimmed the lights and played a scene from *The Truman Show* where Jim Carrey realizes he is living in a false world and decides to brave extreme elements to escape.[1] If you've never seen the movie, it's excellent, just like Jim Carrey always is, but to catch you up: the film is about a man who is trapped in a reality TV show where everyone and everything in his life is pre-planned and created around him. Toward the end of the movie, he begins to realize what is happening and decides he will sail across the "ocean" and find the way out of the production set. As he sails across said ocean, the show's producers give their best efforts to stop him from leaving. They create a storm and throw one thing after another at Jim Carrey's character. There are many points where obstacles are in his path, and he could stop and say, "I can't do this anymore." Instead, he keeps going because he needs change. He wants to get out badly enough that it's more important to him to push through the obstacles than to give in or give up. Spoiler alert: He continues to fight and eventually makes it out, finds the love of his life, and—you guessed it—lives happily ever after.

When the scene ended, the speaker warned us that what we would experience if we chose to make a huge change would be very much like the scene we had just watched, but he also assured us that it would be worth it in the end.

Divorce is so much like that scene. When I was attending this conference, I suspected my marriage was coming to an end soon, even if we hadn't vocalized it yet. I knew, though, in that room, I heard this message for a reason. I knew it was my message to listen to and absorb. I felt that there was going to be something I would have to battle in my life and that it was going to be a massive change. I understood that I would have to put up with the elements that would be thrown at me, and I could not back down from them because I was going to thrive on the other side.

As expected, my divorce played out very much like that scene. Everything around me was used to married Jenn—the standard of "happily ever after" in our society. So, when I started making the changes that come with divorce, I had to battle things that I was unfamiliar with. I encountered extreme and foreign elements along the way. I faced challenges such as custody battles, dividing assets that I never thought I would lose, having emotional conversations I never expected to have with someone I was once in love with, and facing internal emotions I didn't even know existed. At some point, I remembered that message from the conference, and it gave me the strength to keep battling.

The goosebumps I got during that speech in Las Vegas made me realize that while a divorce is one of the scariest things I would ever go through, it was not going to be as frightening as what I perceived the situation to be. In my moment of awareness, I realized a divorce means huge, huge change. For many of us, our goal is that the divorce will be a change for the better. Even though better things may come, we still face the reality that there are many obstacles to overcome to get to the other—and better—side.

DIVORCE BUCKET LIST

I am grateful every day that I didn't back down, that I didn't give up, that I held firm and pushed through. Life on the other side of divorce has turned out to be absolutely beautiful. Your story can be like that, too!

Playing Basketball

After spending twelve years with someone before the online dating era, I'd be a liar if I didn't admit I was at least a little giddy to try the online dating stuff once we separated. You know, time to peruse the previously forbidden goods. It was like going to an all-you-can-eat buffet after eating only salads with lemon juice for years on end. Spoiler Alert: I do not recommend jumping in headfirst—either with online dating or at the buffet after a diet. It just never ends well. In my case, it ended up being a rollercoaster of a rebound where I shattered my already broken heart even more.

Side note: I'm the kind of person that loves explaining a joke after telling it, just to make sure the person really gets it, so I can't help myself here. If you haven't noticed, the title of this chapter is Playing Basketball because it's all about my textbook rebound.

A few weeks after my ex-husband moved out, I decided to give the good ol' Tinder a try. I remembered seeing some of my single friends having their go at it over the years and thought it might be fun to swipe, swipe, swipe. I mean, what could possibly go wrong, right? Turns out, the whole experience set back years and years of confidence-building that I had done for myself. When I first realized my marriage was failing, I started getting into personal development and learning how to be a more confident, centered person—more on that later. I had no clue that what I thought would be a little bit of fun could so quickly unravel so much of that hard work.

The first time I downloaded a dating app, I was lying on my parent's couch, actually feeling confident in the decision to get divorced, but I was seriously lonely. After you live with someone for over a decade, it is a rough adjustment to be alone; you really start to crave another human adult's presence. If you are going through a divorce or separation, I want you to know that this is a totally normal feeling. It's okay to embrace that feeling, but at the end of this chapter, I will give you some tools to cope with these feelings without going through the same downfalls I did.

So, back to the couch: I decided it was time to download Tinder. I was certain I would end up going on a few decent dates and most likely end up falling madly in love again because I was healed, in my mind, and ready—HA!

Having never experienced this technologically advanced dating scene, it was a shock as a woman to feel like I was walking through a club with a sign saying, "Please hit on me! Looking for someone to take me home!" It felt like a mad house, to say the least. I got so overwhelmed within the first hour that I ended up quickly deleting the app. There was this one guy, though, that I had matched with, gotten a message from, had great banter with, and had given my number to before deleting the app. I do not want to share his actual name, but we will call him Alex for the sake of this retelling.

Alex and I started talking almost 24/7 pretty quickly (red flag?), he said *ALL* the right things (red flag?), he was so incredibly hot that I couldn't believe he was talking to little old me—yes, old me, I was seven years his senior (red flag?). After a while, Alex would frequently keep me at a distance. When I would become impatient with the situation and want to run, he would rush in and butter me back up (red flag?).

Listen, I'm not saying all of the above things are always red flags, but what I am saying is that a now-more-rational Jenn who has healed from the trauma of divorce is aware that love doesn't happen overnight. People who want something *real* aren't going to come across so strong at first, only to play mind games with you in the end. If there is ever a time when you are dating someone, and you feel one of the following two things in your gut, please RUN. It might not be easy to do, but you will find happiness elsewhere without putting yourself through the pain—more on that later.

*If your gut tells you the person you are dating isn't super into you because of their actions, or they act hot then cold, then hot then cold, or maybe they say one thing and do another; RUN!

*If you find yourself falling head over heels with the first person that gives you attention, and you want to call it love almost immediately—well ... maybe don't run, but at least take an ice bath and calm the heck down, friend. Real love takes time, and you are probably experiencing a rebound like I was.

I don't fault Alex at all, and while I'll never know whether he was actually one of those infamous "f-boys" or whether I scared him away with my rebounding behavior, I do know that I am wiser for the experience.

I remember the first night I went over to his house. It was, in fact, our first date. Yes, I was so enthralled with this guy and our banter that I went to his place on the first date—insert face palm. As part of our fun banter, he had mentioned that if our first date didn't involve watching some Disney movie I had yet to see, then things wouldn't work out. So, desperate as I was for things to work out, I abandoned my morals and proceeded to put on my favorite makeup, curl my hair, and drive an hour to hang out with him—serial killer or not.

I got to his house, and he was so charming that the now-Jenn would have immediately doubted his intentions. He cooked for me, kissed me at just the right time, and pointed out how much his dogs loved me. We cuddled and watched a movie, he gave me an entirely PG shoulder massage, and then ... then ... he walked me to my car and kissed me goodnight. I was so conflicted because, as a woman who had just gotten out of a marriage where sex was infrequent, I was feeling some pent-up energy, to say the least. I couldn't believe it! This man didn't even have the decency to try to have sex with me— the nerve, haha!!! At the same time, my morals and internal voice were screaming at me about how lucky I was to walk away and how bad things could have gone.

P.S. Don't worry, my friends. Two weeks later, he redeemed himself for his lack of attempt, ending my dry spell.

As I drove home that first night, I remember having butterflies. I wish that someone would have slapped me straight and told me that the butterflies were not the feelings of falling in love; instead, they were the feelings of falling as I was bouncing off a backboard. Oh wait, my bad, I had plenty of friends telling me this man was no good, and I just didn't want to hear it.

I was almost home when I got the text: "I had a really good time with you. No matter how this ends, glad we met." I remember having a gut feeling and focusing on those words: "how this ends." In the back of my mind, I thought that phrase sounded quite ominous. Another hint to trust your gut!

The next few months, I continued talking nonstop with Alex and saw him occasionally, including attending a music festival together and him coming to a wedding with me. There were times where it felt like I was in a fairy tale. He was very smooth. But, at some unknown point, things changed very suddenly. He stopped calling, stopped texting as much, and had excuses not to hang out. I didn't understand because nothing wrong had actually happened. It led to me falling back into my old abandonment issues—stemming from childhood. The further he pulled away, the more I clung to the idea that I couldn't lose "what we had." Part of me didn't think I could bear the rejection because it was on top of the pain that I was already feeling from the divorce, even though I was using a lot of distractions to avoid dealing with that pain.

I didn't realize it until months later, but my discomfort of being alone, which led me to the dating site, was part of my demise. I needed to learn to be alone to be aware of what I wanted and needed in a relationship instead of deciding that I needed just about anyone to fill the void. When you decide you need someone, you can become clingy, unattractive, and straight-up lose your entire self, even if you had previously spent years or decades finding yourself.

After weeks of excuses as to why he couldn't hang out, I finally stood up for myself. I sent him a text letting him know that I didn't understand what changed and that if he couldn't make time for me, he should tell me that. At this point, things had digressed to where he was keeping me around, but with crumbs and distance. He was giving me just enough attention to stick around. I woke up the following morning to a text from him telling me he thought it would be better if we could just be friends. I was devastated.

For weeks, I tried reconciling this rejection. I replayed scenarios over and over in my head, wondering what I could have done differently to change the outcome of his behavior. I bullied myself for being so vulnerable and raw with him. I beat myself up repeatedly for the way I had been so open with my heart and how I had not portrayed myself as someone desirable. I spent way too much time picking apart almost every interaction, reading through our past text conversations again and again. I was lost, broken, and feeling totally rejected. I was not okay.

On the surface, I took that final text from Alex harder than my divorce. Here's why: when I found out I was getting a divorce, the trauma and pain were far too difficult to bear. So, subconsciously, I tried to replace what I had lost. When I lost that replacement, I spiraled because I had no further distractions. I realized I had to face pain, but the pain of losing someone I knew for just months was far easier to face than the pain of a failed marriage with kids involved. I wish I had done the scary thing and just confronted the pain of the divorce before jumping back into dating.

I know now that love, while it's sometimes scary at first, is a fantastic feeling. It should never include feelings of doubt or fear of abandonment. You should be comfortable with yourself and know you can if needed, survive confidently on your own before you enter into a new relationship.

Don't do what I did! Here's what you can do instead…

How to Enjoy Being Alone

1. Take some time to really get to know yourself. Take yourself on a date somewhere you wished your partner would have taken you but never did—or just go out to dinner; it doesn't have to be fancy. While you are there, bring a journal. In your journal, write down five things that you want in the next five years, three things from your past that changed you, and two things about your future that you are excited about.

2. Make a list of what you truly want in a partner—more on this later. What are your non-negotiables? This way, when you are getting to know someone, you will be less likely to settle for anything other than what you want and deserve.

3. Sit alone in a quiet room and allow yourself to simply be in the present. Alone. Just be. Listen to the sounds; think of three things you are grateful for. Do this for ten minutes every day for a week straight. You will start to train yourself to realize that being alone isn't as scary as it feels.

The Bucket List

Looking back on everything, it's clear to me that the process of going through a divorce is a complete journey. It can be a journey that ruins you, or it can be a journey that leads you to a brighter and stronger place in your life. For me, it started as a journey that almost ruined me. There were so many points where I found myself spiraling out of control. At times throughout my experiences in the divorce process, I couldn't even recognize myself.

It's important to give yourself grace, knowing that there may be a point in your journey where you go through downtimes and possibly even feel like things are spiraling out of control. Set an expectation for yourself that you know the divorce journey will not be easy and that at some point, you may even feel as if you are at rock bottom. Then know that you can rebuild from there. Your rock bottom might look different than mine. Your rock bottom might be one day crying in the bathtub with a glass of wine, or it might look like losing everything you've had—friends, family, finances, belongings, maybe even children for a little bit and having to start from scratch. But I need you to know that no matter where your spiral or rock bottom takes you, you are going to come back from it.

The only way a caterpillar turns into a butterfly is by becoming this disgusting, gooey mess inside of a cocoon. If a caterpillar can be completely broken down (literally, tissue is dissolved) and lose its entire identity—the only identity it knew all of its life—then go on to become this majestic, beautiful, flying creature, why can't you do the same? What happens to the caterpillar isn't as crazy as it sounds. It's the same thing that figuratively happens to us in our lives. There are often periods in life when we break down completely from the identity that we knew for ourselves ... divorce is no exception.

When you go through a divorce, you're coming into it with a life that you had envisioned as your forever life. You build so many things together; a family, home, children, a social life, businesses. There are all of these things that you worked so hard in a partnership to create but are now no longer stable existences in your life. There was this expectation that you would live the rest of your life in this world you formed with your partner. With divorce comes the loss of that reality, and that is some heavy shit! In my opinion, it makes total sense why someone would struggle immensely in that situation. I want to give you permission to break down (within reason—don't go too crazy here) so that you can rebuild stronger and rise like a Phoenix because that is what you deserve. As I write this today, I am grateful for the slight breakdowns I'm about to tell you about. I believe that just like a butterfly, I had to have breakdowns and struggles to be who I am and love the way I love now. I don't believe I truly learned to love fully until after going through my divorce.

THE ATTACK

By the time my divorce started, I was already battling crippling panic attacks. I literally couldn't even drive my car. I knew if I was going to step out into this world as a single person again, be independent, and get through this battle, then I was going to have to face my panic and anxiety head-on.

I'll never forget my very first panic attack.

A few months before my anxiety and panic disorders made their grand entrance, I arrived home from a work trip to something unimaginable. I had called home a few times while I was on this trip and was told that everything was going well with the kids and at home. I had arranged for my mother-in-law to pick me up from the airport. We were going to grab the kids from daycare before she dropped us off at home. My now ex-husband and I were going to have a family dinner then.

When I arrived home, I found the house smelled of mildew, there were water stains on the ceilings, and the carpets on the first floor were completely soaked. My husband was nowhere to be found. I tried to call him, but he wouldn't answer his phone. Hours later, he finally texted me and told me he was staying at a friend's house that night. I had no clue what happened to create this disaster I had walked in on.

I later found out that my now ex-husband had flooded the house. He had turned the bathtub on and forgot it was running, left the house, and came back to find it flooded hours later. I was also informed that he told people I had angrily scolded him for the incident, so they would help him try to cover it up. I hadn't even known anything had happened at the point that he told this lie to people. But listen, we all make mistakes, all kinds of errors. I can understand that, as I had indeed made my fair share of mistakes in the marriage. What I really couldn't understand were the false accusations and lack of communication. It was an actual, blatant breakdown of our marriage vows. I had wanted out of the marriage for years by this point, but this moment was when I knew that our marriage was over on his end, too. It was now a ticking time bomb.

My now ex-husband didn't come home at all that day. Left alone with the kids, I leaped into action. There was no way we could stay in the house because of the mildew, so I found a hotel, called the insurance company, and started getting everything in order. By the end of the whole ordeal, half of our entire home ended up needing to be gutted and refinished. It was a very stressful experience as we moved into a hotel—and later into his parents' house—with our entire family, including two pets. Battling insurance companies and contractors over details, figuring out the financial side, and preparing for an unexpected remodel while also juggling daily life added to that stress. The word stress doesn't even start to cover it.

A month after we finally moved back in, my grandmother passed away. It was only a few days before Thanksgiving when I got the call. My mom had called to tell me that my grandmother, who suffered from Alzheimer's, was actively passing. She said it could be a day or a few days; they didn't know. My parents live a few hours away, so I proceeded to head their way. I sat with my father at Grandma's bedside because he didn't want to leave her, and I didn't want to leave him.

Grandma was always stubborn, I get that from her, and so it took a while for her to give up her fight. I sat by her bedside with my dad for three full days, not eating, hardly sleeping, and witnessing one of the most traumatic things I've ever observed in my life. Seeing the human body deteriorate as it passes is not something I would wish on anyone. Can I give a huge long-distance hug to all the nurses, doctors, and medical professionals that deal with this on a routine basis? You are all heroes!

That experience is something that still haunts me to this day. It's no wonder, looking back now, that as I drove back to my hometown for Christmas a few weeks later, I had my very first panic attack. It came on so suddenly. Although I always had forms of anxiety, I never had a full-blown panic attack before. I didn't even understand what panic attacks really were before experiencing one myself. If you have panic attacks, you know that they're one of the most terrifying things that can happen to your body.

By this point, my husband and I were basically living separate lives as the marriage continued to implode, so when the panic attack hit, it was just the kids and me in the car. Almost two hours into the ride, my youngest decided, right after we'd passed the part of the trip where all of the bathroom stops were, that he had to use the bathroom; pretty typical for a four-year-old, right?! So, I pulled over on the side of the road when I found a spot that seemed safe.

I told him to open his door because the field was on his side. Once there was a clearing in traffic on my side, I opened my door, so I could step around and help him.

What happened next was a blur. Suddenly, my heart started pounding through my chest. I collapsed against my side of the car because I'd gotten so dizzy and weak that I couldn't stand straight anymore. I quickly jumped back into the car, having no idea what was happening to my body. As my left arm started going numb, the only thing I could think was, "This is it, I'm having a heart attack, and I'm going to die in front of my children."

After that, I couldn't control any thoughts in my head. I couldn't feel anything in my body. My neck, my shoulders, and the back of my head tensed up completely. I had this throbbing pain in my head like it was going to explode. I couldn't associate with my body. It was like I was sitting on top of the car watching this all happen. I realized I couldn't possibly drive to get help. I somehow found a way to call my mom and describe what was going on.

At this point, I was probably about forty-five minutes from their house, so my father and my step-uncle jumped in a car to come up and meet me. Those were the longest forty-five minutes of my life. At that time, I had no clue what a panic attack was, and I was terrified. As I waited, I gave my oldest son my phone and told him, "If Mommy passes out, call 911. Tell them what is on the signs that you see." Then I sat there, just trying to maintain consciousness and praying I wasn't dying right in front of my children. I didn't want them to experience that.

By the time my dad arrived, I was sick to my stomach and shaking uncontrollably. I couldn't control my body at all. I spent a couple of hours in the bathroom at the ER as we waited for them to take me back. The whole time I was waiting, I kept thinking, "What are they doing? Can't they see I'm dying?" When they finally took me back, they sat me in a room and told me I had a panic attack and that everything would be okay. They gave me some medicine and sent me on my way. I had no clue that those panic attacks were going to become part of my everyday life. Every time I had another panic attack—they came almost daily for a while—I was left feeling crippled and soon started fearing nearly everything around me.

For over a year after that first attack, it would happen again every time I got in a car. While none of the panic attacks were as bad as the first one, they were bad enough that I ended up back in the ER four more times within three months until I finally believed that I wasn't going to die on the spot. I became so fearful of driving that I avoided it at all costs and eventually did not drive at all. You can imagine that this put a lot of strain on our already failing marriage. So, when we decided to start the separation, I decided to get serious about my health and stop letting this crippling anxiety control my life. Instead, I decided to start listening to the doctors. I finally started medication for anxiety disorder. While I'm not proud to say that I take something, I'm grateful to have my life back.

I started seeing a therapist. I genuinely hope that everyone can get over any type of stigma around therapy and do that for themselves, too, because if I hadn't done that, I would not have addressed my childhood trauma. I also would not have healed from the trauma of being married to an addict nor the trauma of the divorce.

From there, I also decided to stop drinking caffeine and alcohol. Number one, they both can cause heart palpitations, which trigger panic attacks. And number two, I thought it would probably be a good idea to have a super clear mind knowing I was about to experience one of the most traumatic things in my life. We can't always predict traumatic things happening in our lives, but when you see something like divorce coming, you can at least prepare your mind and mental state a little bit. After the scare in my parents' pool, followed by the onset of panic attacks, it was time to clear my head and make significant changes. I wasn't going to lean on a glass of wine to ease my fears, and I wouldn't have my favorite IPA—or three—to deal with the depression; instead, I needed to hero the heck up and face the things I was about to go through so that I could grow from them.

THE WEIGHT

While I was starting to take action to resolve my anxiety disorder, it was still not entirely under control at the beginning of our divorce process. Once the divorce began, there were many weeks, maybe even months, where I couldn't move. I couldn't function. I was literally the walking dead as I went through my life. Many things happened during that time that I don't even remember happening. There were friendships made and lost, we battled over custody of the children, there were endless appointments with lawyers, I lost my family dog, and I've probably even forgotten other things that happened. There were days where I even questioned if I would ever be happy or normal again.

I had suspected that the divorce was coming for years because both of us were very unhappy. But I'm the kind of person that values commitment, so I would never have initiated divorce on my own. Once he said he wanted it, though, I felt a huge weight come off of my shoulders. I knew it was the right thing for us, and, in the end, it would be best for the kids, too. Knowing it was the right thing still did not make it any less painful. As I said, my entire world was about to change, and one of the scariest things in the world is the fear of the unknown. The unknown can render you completely motionless.

Leading up to facing the unknown territories of divorce, I had done years of work on my mind. I had prepared myself for dealing with the divorce by building a support system of friends and family, paying more attention to my health, reading self-development books, and receiving coaching and counseling. Still, that work did not make me thoroughly prepared.

So, naturally, at some point, I went into an absolute downward spiral.

Shortly after my ex-husband moved out, we started battling over custody of the children. There were explicit reasons based on my ex-husband's past that I had specific requests regarding custody, but those are part of his story and are not my details to share at this point. At the time, my intentions were purely surrounding my children's safety. Don't get me wrong, he loves those kids and was always an interactive father with them; there was never any violence, and he was present as a dad. I will never take that from him, but I was afraid. The custody disagreements were some of the hardest things for all of us.

As we started to go through the custody situation, I became unable to sleep. My panic started creeping back in again. By then, I had gone months without a panic attack, and I was so proud of myself because I had almost daily attacks before that. It seemed like all of the work I had done and the changes I had made were paying off. Yet as we approached this phase of the divorce, all of the symptoms of my panic disorder suddenly came back.

I was running my own business from home at that time, and I began noticing changes in my work ethic. I was going from complete slay mode to slowly losing control of my business. There were days when if I didn't have my children, I didn't get out of bed. I laid there thinking, "This isn't fair. A mother should never go a day without seeing her young children. It's not fair." And, the truth is, you guys, it's not fair at all, not in the least bit, but I promise you that you *can* rebuild something beautiful from it. I laid in bed feeling like I was a failure as a mother because I couldn't make my relationship with their father work and that I'd done them some horrible injustice in their life. I worried about all the what-ifs and how the divorce would affect my kids in the future.

Why did I worry so much? Now, years later, I can tell you that they are the happiest kids in the world. I'm sure there are minor impacts that they will carry with them through life from it. But, if we had stayed married, they probably would have much larger baggage to bear from the toxic relationship around them. I eventually learned that I'd rather they have little breaks from Mommy and Daddy than witness behavior that would cause them to think that the relationship we had was acceptable. I want my boys to know love and to have peace. I want to be that role model for them by showing them what a healthy, loving relationship looks like.

During all of this worrying, I ended up losing about forty pounds, which, usually, I wouldn't complain about. But it got to the point where family and friends were making comments. I realized I was going days without eating.

When I was younger, a senior in high school, I began to suffer from multiple eating disorders. Being the perfectionist, overachiever that I am, I couldn't just pick one eating disorder. I decided that I was going to have both anorexia and bulimia.

Growing up, I was always referred to as the "fat kid" in my group of friends. Family members would call me fat and make ongoing comments about my weight. While I was by no means the skinniest girl in my grade, I also wouldn't say that I was obese or even that much overweight. I was always athletic and played multiple sports. Speaking of sports, I once had a biology teacher tell me that he could understand why I was the catcher for our fast pitch softball team because most catchers were "chunky like me." When we played powder-puff football, some of my "best friends" referred to me as the "fat little lineman." It was their loving nickname for me throughout high school. Maybe it was all in fun for them, but, for me, it had lasting effects.

Starting in high school, I slowly developed a form of anorexia, but it wasn't super noticeable to others. As a matter of fact, I don't think anyone noticed it while I was in high school. I believe that is because I had just gotten my first serious boyfriend, so losing weight when you're "in love" is expected.

A year later, I went off to college. While there, I became a perfectionist in so many ways. I ended up graduating college with two degrees and a 3.98 GPA, which tells you how much I throw myself into things that I dedicate myself to. That being said, I didn't leave any dedication untouched to my eating disorders. I would wake up in the morning and go to class. I would look at the clock all day long because I had a goal. I would not let myself eat until 2 p.m. That was the magical time when I would allow myself to have my one meal of the day. It was like my personal game with myself. When I reached that time, I would typically get a sandwich of some kind, and then that was it for the day.

The attention I started receiving as I was losing weight was only positive reinforcement for my crazy eating behavior. I was getting more attention from guys. Friends were telling me I was looking amazing. I was succeeding in college, became super involved in activities, and, to me, somehow that all was happening because I was "conquering my weight." To me, if I was skinny, then I was successful. If I wasn't skinny, everything else in my life would fall apart.

It breaks my heart looking back at that little girl who thought her entire worth centered around her weight.

Slowly, the eating disorder began to progress because with college comes drinking, and with drinking comes eating late-night pizza. After a bit, I started working out seven days a week for three hours a day. Then, naturally, I added throwing up every single meal I ate into the mix. There was a point during my college career where my parents almost hospitalized me, and they gave me an ultimatum—if I didn't start eating and gaining back some weight, they were going to do something about it themselves.

Looking back at pictures now, I can't believe the extent of the body dysmorphia I had. What I see is this struggling, skinny, anorexic young woman who thought she was fat, obese, and unworthy but was still somehow succeeding in life because she was in control of the numbers on the scale and what she was eating.

I was still battling my eating disorders when my now ex-husband and I met the year after graduating from college. We met in May of that year through mutual friends. We were engaged in August of the same year, and, by that same September, we had moved into a tiny apartment together. Two weeks after moving in together, we found out we were pregnant. Throughout my pregnancy, I was still battling my eating disorders. I suffered from things that had happened to me during my childhood, and I was broken. It wouldn't be until years later that I would be able to address and work through my demons to finally beat my eating disorders and accept myself for who I am.

Now I realize that at the start of my divorce, I was spiraling back into the old habits of my eating disorders. Of course, my family and friends were severely concerned when I dropped all that weight super quickly. I didn't see it at the time, but I'm glad that people brought it to my attention because I had worked so hard to beat my eating disorders.

As soon as everyone started voicing their concerns to me, I became self-aware. The moment I knew things were getting out of control was when my counselor told me that my only homework from her was to go home and eat all of my favorite foods. I was breaking down before transforming. I decided I did not come this far only to backtrack. I'm glad that I was able to catch and pull myself out of that spiral and get back on track with my eating.

THE CONTRACT

At one point, several months after the divorce was filed, I felt so lost that I started turning to all of the easy outs. I began drinking again. I was on Tinder way more than I would like to admit, and I was putting myself in some pretty questionable situations. I started losing friends because I wasn't present for them. I was so absorbed in my own battles and self-pity that I wasn't able to be there the way those friends deserved.

I remember one cringe-worthy day in particular. In hindsight, this is probably a little bit of a funny story, but it was also a wake-up moment for me in my journey. I tell this story now because I look back on it and realize my coping mechanisms were getting out of control.

On a particularly hot day in the summer, I decided to go tubing with one of my girlfriends—just the two of us without kids. We brought a couple of beverages, headed down to the river, and floated for three hours. We shared divorce stories, and, by the end, we were a little bit tipsy.

Once I got home, I was invited to a neighbor's cookout, where I continued to drink. At this point, getting on Tinder, swiping, and feeling wanted was one of the only things I was leaning on to pick up my self-esteem. I should have been relying on my business, family, and knowledge of my own worth instead. At this low, the only thing that made me feel like I had any value was sexual attention from men.

I was sitting at this cookout with my neighbors, swiping on Tinder, when I noticed the profile of a guy from LA who said he was currently staying in the area. I thought he would make for fun conversation, so I swiped right. He messaged me immediately, telling me he was in town visiting friends and family. He divulged that he was from this area but had recently moved out to California. He said that he didn't have any plans that night and asked if I would be willing to meet up at a bar for a drink.

I'd already had a few beverages, so the liquid courage was coursing through me. The bar we ended up meeting at was only two minutes from my house, so I took an Uber to get there. It was my first time meeting a guy from a dating app in a bar. At the time, to me, it was an adventure.

I walked into the bar and, surprisingly, felt immediately at ease with this guy. He was super fun, and there was no pressure. In another life, we probably would have been great friends! We had an incredible time. Eventually, we got to the part of the night where he asked if I wanted to go back to his friend's house with him. Again, that liquid courage mixed with the need to feel like I was worth something crept back in.

I had been having a good time, so I decided I would go back with him. But I wanted to make sure I wasn't going to compromise my safety. I mean, I hardly knew this guy, so I'd already taken all the standard safety precautions of online dating—my friends knew where I was, and I had my location turned on in my phone. Still, in my inebriated state, that wasn't enough for me.

I made this poor guy promise he wasn't going to harm me and that if anything happened to me, he would pay my children $500 a month for the rest of his life. Whoever this crazy version of me was that night decided a verbal agreement wasn't enough. I then had the bartender give me a piece of paper and a pen, and I proceeded to draw up an official contract.

The contract had both of our names, the terms and conditions, signature lines for both of us, a signature line for the witness—the bartender in this case, and probably some remnants of booze smeared on it. We were all laughing and making a joke out of it. I took a picture of the contract and sent it to my girlfriends, and we all had a little laugh as well. Later, we joked that it might be an excellent idea for an app.

After our contract was completed, I headed back with him to his friend's house. We had the place to ourselves all night, and I will tell you, even though it was pretty out of character and I'm glad it was a one-time type of behavior, it was one of the most fun nights I've had with a guy. We spent the entire night going through a cycle of insanely fun and wild sex to deep conversations about life to back to the wild sex, over and over again. We stayed up all night, and, during one of the conversations, I even found myself being comforted in his arms as I cried to him, finally letting my emotions about the divorce release fully. I felt vulnerable, but in a good way, and he offered so much support and companionship. I cannot thank him enough for that night; while it was out of character for me, I do not regret it in any way, and I am grateful for that turning point in my journey and for him being so understanding and fun throughout it.

There were times when I questioned including this story in this book for fear of judgment. In the end, I included it because I decided it is important for myself and others to let go of the shame sometimes associated with fulfilling human needs. I realize that even though it was a very enjoyable night for me, I did have some shame attached because of societal standards and judgments. I also recognize that if the gender roles were reversed, there would be very little to no judgment or shame, so I am deciding to release any guilt I felt for acting on my desires that night. I encourage everyone to do the same as they heal, within reason, of course! Stay safe out there, folks!

The following day when I woke up, he drove me home, and he was an absolute gentleman. When I look back on that night, I realize that it could have gone wrong in so many ways. It didn't, and I think the night happened because I needed to reach my total reset point. When I got home the next morning, I was grateful for that connection because I believe there are different reasons people come into our lives. I think that connection was there to give me what I needed that day, which was a fun time and a little bit of letting go. Mostly, I needed a wake-up call to stop my self-pity and disastrous behavior and start rebuilding who I am, what I truly deserve, and what I am capable of. That is precisely what I got that day.

I ran into my house, threw myself down on the couch, and said out loud, "What are you doing, Jenn? This isn't you." I knew that, deep down, the real me was still there. The real me craves bonds and commitments, not one-night stands. Even though I had enjoyed the experience for what it was, I realized that I was acting like a stranger to my own self. I had also unlocked the gates to let out the emotions I held in for so long and knew that I couldn't go back. At this point, though the experience was unforgettable and I was grateful for it, I realized I was more than a little lost.

When they say that you have to hit your true bottom before you can start to rebuild and become a better person, they mean it. I realized that I wasn't doing this divorce thing correctly. Something needed to change. If I didn't change my approach and focus, I was going to spiral completely out of control.

I needed to stop breaking down; it was time for me to start rebuilding and become the butterfly.

THE LIST

On a gorgeous summer night, I was porch-gossiping with a friend. I was telling them how I was struggling. I told them I knew I needed to change something because I was completely losing myself. I let my friend know I wasn't sure I was worthy of ever being loved again. I was so down on myself, some of that because when you're in a relationship that's going downhill, hurtful things can be said on both sides, and words are damaging. The words I endured injured me severely. I was in a really, really bad place.

I know I said more than a fair share of damaging things to my ex-husband; I think it can tend to happen when a relationship enters the toxic phase, and I genuinely hope that he has found a way to heal from the words I said to him. There are specific words that I carried with me, from his side, for a very long time, and those words caused me to self-sabotage because I believed them so much. The phrase that damaged me entirely was something he said at our last dinner together.

Back before he officially filed for divorce, my now ex-husband asked if we could sit down to dinner together to try to come up with an agreement for our separation. I had loved the idea of trying to save money during the divorce, so I agreed to attempt to negotiate and find a solution together. We decided, trying to be amicable, to go to dinner at one of our favorite restaurants in town to discuss the terms.

We rode to dinner together, doing our best to remain cordial. After we ordered our meals, we decided to get down to business. It turned out that my now ex-husband wasn't looking to discuss and develop an arrangement together. Instead, he had laid out his terms and wanted me to sign documents on the spot. Feeling completely blind-sided and misled on the purpose of this conversation, I told him that I would need to discuss his terms with my lawyer before deciding anything. He was not happy with this response, and the cordial mood suddenly dissolved.

Still waiting for our food, he asked me, "Do you think this divorce is the right thing?"

"No, not at all," I responded sadly, because I was terrified of the impact on our children and afraid of the unknown, fully committed to the *'til death do us part* aspect of our vows.

He then discussed reasons that he thought it was the right thing to do, and somehow the conversation got tense along the way. At one point, despite him knowing me better than anyone else and therefore knowing about the deep-seated abandonment issues I had, the following words came out of his mouth:

"You don't have any real friends. All you have is fake internet friends. Anyone that truly gets to know you and who you really are leaves you."

I'm so proud of myself for what I did next. I had heard similar phrases from him over the years, typically resulting in me crying alone in my bedroom. But, this time, I stood up, grabbed the paperwork he had laid on the table for me to sign, put it in my purse, and said, "You will NEVER say those words to me again." I walked out of the restaurant, passing the waitress as she was bringing the food to the table.

Standing alone on the street outside of the restaurant, I called an Uber to get home because we had ridden to the restaurant in my now ex-husband's car. Once I got home, I immediately called my best friend to tell her what had happened and was still on the phone with her when my now ex-husband returned hours later.

DIVORCE BUCKET LIST

A little later that night, I went to check on the kids and noticed my now ex-husband was standing in the bathroom, just staring into the mirror, as if he was searching for an answer that was hidden somewhere on his face.

That night, once the kids were asleep, he silently packed his bags and left for good.

Sitting on the porch a few months after that, I told my friend that I had no clue how I was going to rebuild my life. I had thought I had always been good at picking myself up since, at this point, I had learned how to cope with anxiety and panic. I had learned how to pick myself back up, but this was deeper than that. This place I was in was the lowest I'd ever been in my life. I don't know how my friend and I came up with the idea that changed everything for me—the idea that saved me—but we did.

Whatever way we stumbled upon it, what we decided was to make a list for me. This friend knew me so well that they knew I lived my life by lists. Seriously, I wake up in the morning, and I don't do anything unless it's on a list. Brush my teeth? Better be on the list—just kidding—I'm not that extreme, but I am definitely a list lover.

This particular list would be made up of things I could focus on and complete, making me start accomplishing positive things for myself again. These things would bring me some joy in small amounts and give me back some self-independence. Eventually, these things would harbor more extensive feelings of empowerment and self-confidence. These activities would lead me to rediscover myself again. I would create experiences that would help me find the love of myself and life again.

And thus, the Divorce Bucket List was born.

Creating Your Divorce Bucket List

I work very hands-on with my clients to create their own Divorce Bucket Lists, which we then work through in an action-based coaching approach. I love watching them rebuild and grow through this process to step back into their confidence and the desires they've dreamed of through and after their divorce! It's incredible to see how others can follow the same process I did to leave survival mode behind and start thriving again! Here are some of the questions we work on together to come up with ideas to add to their Divorce Bucket List. You can use these questions to jog your brain on your dreams and desires and create your own list, too!

Step 1 - Pull out a piece of paper and write down your answers to the below questions:

- If I could start a new hobby, it would be:
- Something I used to enjoy doing but haven't done in a while is:
- If I could reconnect to people who I lost touch with, they would be:
- If I could spend more time with certain friends/family, they would be:

- Some of the things I've always wanted to do but just haven't done yet are:
- If I could take myself on a date for a day just to take care of myself and feel completely happy, that ideal day would look like this:
- A fear I would like to overcome is:
- I would feel super successful if I accomplished this:

Step 2 – Using the questions above, pick the top five things you would like to add to your Divorce Bucket List and write them on a separate piece of paper.

Voila! You now have your own Divorce Bucket List, so you can start working through small steps to achieve the items on your list. Once you read on to see how much this list helped me in my journey, you will be so ready to dive right into taking action on your list items, too!!

> **Book Bonus:** You can get access to a free printable work-sheet for creating your Divorce Bucket List here:
>
> **go.divideguide.com/worksheet**

Must-Do Mama

I knew that if I was going to truly set out to be a stronger and better version of myself through and after my divorce, I would have to figure out what I desired in life and then treat those goals as non-negotiables. I dedicated myself to learning from people who had overcome and thrived in their goals, people who had these insane mindsets that could accomplish anything they put their mind to. As I studied these people and their minds, I found that they didn't accomplish insane things because they were any better than someone else. They did it because they trained their minds to be goal-oriented. Once that clicked for me, I knew it was time to become goal-oriented too, so I could get myself through the most traumatic thing I'd ever faced. I didn't just want to survive it but instead, find a way to turn it into a positive growth experience.

One of the traits I noticed about these successful people was that they have what I like to call a "Must-Do Mindset" about the things they want to achieve. This trait isn't something we are given; it's all based on the choices we make. Here's the crazy thing: we all have had that Must-Do Mindset about something we have really wanted at some point in our lives. It comes down to what you are applying that Must-Do Mindset towards. When you enter your Must-Do Mindset, you go from thinking, "*Can* this happen?" to "*How* will I make this happen?" and then you overcome any obstacle thrown at you to make your desired outcome a reality. Think about it, if it's a super hot summer day, and all you want in the entire world that day is a cold, refreshing ice cream cone, you are going to do what it takes to get that ice cream cone.

Imagine this: it's 102 degrees outside, hot as Hell, and you want some ice cream so badly that you can already taste it and feel the cold treat resting on your tongue. You go to your freezer to grab your treat and notice someone must have finished the ice cream you bought last week because there's no ice cream in your freezer. You have your mind set on this ice cream, so you don't just go back outside into the heat.

Instead, you get in your car because you know a place down the road with the best ice cream. You put your keys into the ignition and then turn the keys, except your car sputters and doesn't start. You think to yourself, "Well, this sucks!" You could just go inside and call it quits, but it's still so hot, and your mouth is watering. You've already decided to get that ice cream, so you call up your best friend. "Hey, bestie, we need to go get ice cream; I'm not taking no for an answer. I need this ice cream. It's 102 degrees out, and all I can think about is chocolate ice cream."

Your bestie is wondering why they didn't think about doing this already, so they come over, pick you up, and together you drive to the ice cream shop. As you pull into a parking space, you notice the lights aren't on, and there is a sign saying it's closed for business. At this point, you've come this far—too far not to get some ice cream—so you redirect your bestie to another place you know of ten minutes down the road. It's going to take you ten more minutes to get it, but it's going to be worth it because it's so hot outside, and you need that ice cream.

You get to the second shop, and it's open! You walk inside and realize that in all of the madness, you forgot your wallet. Now what? You must have that ice cream; you can almost taste it, so you can't walk away now. At this point, you realize you have two acceptable options, and not getting ice cream is definitely not one of them. You can borrow money from your friend and pay them back, or you can have them drive you back home to grab your wallet and come back. Either way, you are getting that ice cream. You decide to borrow the money from your friend because you *must* have this ice cream now.

You finally have your ice cream, and even though you didn't get it via the easy path you first envisioned, it actually tastes better than you imagined because of the hard work you put in to get it. It's refreshing, delicious, and totally hits the spot.

Getting your cold treat probably took an hour or so longer than expected, and there were tons of obstacles to overcome, but you had already committed to the decision, so the challenges didn't stop you.

Going through a divorce and redefining your new life is a lot like that.

You will define your new goals, desires, and dreams, and then you will hit obstacle after obstacle on the way there. You have to do a little mindset work to develop a Must-Do Mindset toward your desires and goals so that when obstacles pop up, they aren't as threatening. When you do this and hit those first few obstacles, instead of saying, "That's it, I give up," you will find solutions because you aren't going to accept anything less than what you desire and deserve. If you had to walk to get to your ice cream, you would have done that because you wanted it badly enough. You have to go after the things you desire the same way you would go after that ice cream; if you have to walk to get to them, then walk!

One of the things I decided to do as part of my Divorce Bucket List was to redefine and discover who I was as a single mom of two boys. I wanted to make sure I could prove to myself that I could be the mom they deserved and endure the challenges of being a single parent. So, I added "Take the boys on vacation alone" to my list.

When I was married, I remember looking at single moms and being absolutely in awe of them. How could they possibly stay sane or even feed themselves while taking care of children on their own, without the help of someone else? I knew that even with a husband, raising children requires so much effort, time, and patience. As a mom, I barely felt like I had time for myself, even with a partner to help. I had no clue how these single moms were doing it; they were my superheroes. Little did I know, though, that I would soon become one of them.

It's crazy that when you look at your superheroes or mentors, the people you admire most, you often can't picture yourself in their position or their situation. Don't be surprised if one day you end up where they are. Be prepared!

Don't be afraid; things will work out the way they're meant to. You might look at someone and think that you could never do what they do, but you will never know unless you're in their shoes. You'll be surprised at what you can achieve. I am happier now as a single mom than I was when I was in an unhappy marriage with a partner to help me.

I won't lie. At first, one of the most brutal struggles was the day my children would leave to go to their dad's house. It was always extremely difficult to know I wouldn't see them for a few days. I would worry about what I might miss and if they would miss me. I'd worry that I wasn't there to protect them or guide them to make the right choices, but more than that, it just didn't feel natural.

So, at first, on the days where they would head to their father's, I would be rendered to sitting alone on my couch, crying for hours until I fell asleep. Eventually, that changed to me being grateful, knowing their father is present in their life, that they have the time to get different life experiences, and that I had time for myself again.

I started to refocus and use this newly freed up time to learn new hobbies, focus on things that made my life better, and, most importantly, self-care. Now, when my children leave to go to their dad's, I watch my favorite TV show, read a book, or jump in a nice warm bath, which is one of my favorite places in the world—lots of bubbles, please. I start our time apart by taking care of myself. Sometimes, I even order takeout for one when they leave—I know, colossal risk-taker here. I just make sure I do something to reset, recharge, and set a positive tone for the time apart.

More than just fearing the time apart, I was unsure how I would juggle being a single mom, working, and keeping up with daily life. My family doesn't live close to me, so I have very limited help when it comes to physical support with my children. When my boys are home with me, I am on 100 percent parental duty, nurse duty, janitor duty, and cafeteria duty—pretty sure growing boys eat enough to set consecutive and ever-growing world records. I don't have to keep explaining; I know any parent reading this is well aware of the many hats that single parents wear! I wouldn't trade it for the world, but it was definitely an adjustment. There is no more splitting up duties once the decision to divorce is made.

When I realized how big of a change I was facing, I knew I needed to take some actions to put myself into a Must-Do Mindset. I needed to prove to myself that I could achieve the thing I was most afraid of as a mom, and I decided I needed to empower myself as a single parent so that the obstacles wouldn't feel as big. I had always been terrified of traveling alone with my children. If you think about it, there are so many things that could go wrong. Not to mention how exhausting it can be taking any family vacation—let alone a single mom family vacation! By putting a family vacation on my Divorce Bucket List, I decided that I would show myself and the world that I could do this scary thing.

If you are entering into single parenthood, your "empowering single parent activity" doesn't have to be as dramatic as mine. You could take a single-parent vacation somewhere less extreme, go camping for the weekend, or do something super easy and affordable like a day trip somewhere local. All you need to do is prove to yourself that you are an amazing parent, you're strong, you've got this, and you can handle the children without a partner. Even parenting solo, your children are going to be happy, safe, taken care of, and feel secure with you as their sole provider for the time they are with you.

When I do something, I kind of tend to go all-in. So, I whipped out my Must-Do Mindset and proceeded to book us a ten-day Disney vacation. Plus, if I was going to do this, I was going to enjoy it at least a little bit! Disney is my absolute favorite place in the world. I knew I could kill two birds with one stone by feeding my soul with Disney magic and also empowering myself as a single mom. I spent a lot of time researching for the trip, which brought me joy as well. Planning a Disney vacation is one of the most fun things you can do, ever—in my opinion, at least. It took a lot of resourcefulness to figure out the trip, financially and logistically, but I was determined.

While our Disney vacation was the kids' fourth one, it was by far the best one I had been on with them. There were times when I felt overwhelmed because two little boys and Disney can be full of activity and take a lot of energy. But I felt so empowered by the fact that there was no drama, no arguing, and the entire trip was full of joy for my boys. We were able to take things slowly and enjoy all of the moments, and I think most of that was because I was purposeful in my intentions of making sure I didn't forget a single memory from that trip.

One of my favorite moments on that trip took place one day while we were at Animal Kingdom. We were about halfway into the day when what felt like a monsoon came through (that sometimes happens if you ever travel to Disney in the peak heat of

August—speaking of wanting an ice cream cone). It started storming so badly that almost every attraction in the park was temporarily closed. The only attractions open were the indoor attractions with extremely long waits because everyone was flocking indoors.

We ran to get on one of our favorite rides—Dinosaur!—only to find the line was over two hours long. We quickly re-routed on a whim and started looking for something else to do inside. We stumbled upon a little, almost hidden shack for some snacks and cute Disney drinks and had the best time with our Mickey cookies and themed drinks. We spent the whole time laughing and watching the storm from the windows of the shack while interacting with some of the friendliest "cast members" I've ever had the pleasure to meet. They kept bringing the boys little treats and filled the experience with magic.

Once the storm had passed, we ventured back outside and ended up following one of the characters around the park, interacting with them as we went and laughing harder than we ever had. The boys found it so funny that their mom was so excited, and they loved running around like they were in a movie themselves! I think this was my favorite memory because it proved I could face a challenge with my kids and still hero up as a solo parent. Instead of letting the torrential downpour ruin our day or even bring it to a halt, we turned the could-be-disaster into magical memories.

One of my favorite pictures of my boys is from that trip. In the picture, we are standing in front of the castle in Magic Kingdom with the purest of smiles and large auras of joy around us. Two years later, we still talk about that trip on a pretty regular basis, and every time my kids start to bring it up with: "Hey, Mom! Remember that time we were in Disney and...." I begin to tear up a little. Sometimes they start that sentence after I've had a particularly challenging day, and I realize that everything will be okay because I can do this. And so can you! Anything that is thrown our way in this new life can be conquered, and we can use this time to become even better versions of ourselves, living even better versions of our lives.

TIPS FOR DEVELOPING A MUST-DO MINDSET

- Imagine yourself having already achieved the goals and desires you have set for yourself. What does it look like? What does it feel like? Close your eyes and literally put yourself in the situation you want to be in. How would you act? How would you feel? What would you do? Once you visualize, in full detail, what it feels like to have that desired outcome, you will be more connected to doing whatever it takes to get there.

- Surround yourself with people that mirror what you want. Don't know who that might be? Try thinking of who has what you want and read their books, get coaching, and take courses. Know people in your life that have the outcomes you want? Grab coffee with them, hang out with them, and learn from them. The more you surround yourself with the people who are and have done what you want to do, the more you will ramp up that Must-Do Mindset.

- Consider the worst-case scenario if you didn't reach your goal. What does that feel like? What does that look like? If the worst-case scenario did happen, what could you do to get things back on track toward your goal—like grabbing a friend to help out in the ice cream story above? Sometimes we hold ourselves back from that Must-Do Mindset because we are afraid of failure. It helps to check ourselves and realize that the "failure" we are so scared of is actually, in most cases, something we can overcome.

- Have positive self-talk. Keep reminding yourself that you ARE going to do this, it HAS to happen, and you DESERVE it!

Here I Go Again, On My Own

It wasn't just the kids that I had to learn how to deal with on my own; I also had to learn how to deal with myself. I was accustomed to being one piece of a partnership for over twelve years; I wasn't sure how to function as a sole entity. I knew I had to challenge myself and push myself outside of my comfort zone to become confident as a single person again. So, I decided to start dating myself and treating myself the way I wanted. I knew it would be no easy feat; I can be quite a handful. I decided to add a few things to my Divorce Bucket List to become self-reliant and really step out on my own again—in conviction.

Minus One

I remember the last outing we did as a family of four.

We knew that things were coming to an end. It had been months since my now ex-husband voiced that he wanted to get a divorce. He'd been living in a separate room in our house for months by this point, and we had been back and forth trying to work it out, but we knew it was over—we just hadn't filed yet.

My oldest son's school held a heritage event where families hosted booths representing different cultures. Full of food and activities, it was a pretty popular event at his school. I'll never forget that day. Probably because we often don't realize when the "last time" is going to happen, much like the last kiss or the last time you hang out with a friend before losing touch with them. Sometimes lasts just happen, and you never really get to sit there and say, "Okay, this is going to be the last time this happens." Sometimes things just fade away and never happen again.

This wasn't like that. My gut told me this was the last time we would be going out on an outing as a family of four; it was certainly bittersweet. I knew this was the last time we would drive in a single car to an event, the last time we would enter that event together, and the last time we would leave together. The craziest thing, though, was that it was the most peaceful experience we'd had in a long time. That peace was the part that made it bittersweet. It almost tricked me into thinking, "Maybe this will be okay... Maybe we could make this work."

Those thoughts were undoubtedly a trick. It was only a few weeks later that the situation went even further south, and there was no repairing the marriage.

When you're used to doing things as a family unit, it can be shocking to start venturing out on your own. I remember how massively intimidating it was at the beginning. I had been used to doing all kinds of events, outings, activities, and holidays as a family unit. Having to transition from that to doing it alone or as a single mom with kids without that partner with you is quite an intimidating situation to face. Time has since passed, now I have gotten used to, and even enjoy, being on my own with the kids during our outings with just the three of us. I would be lying, though, if I didn't admit it was hard in the beginning. Specifically, one outing comes to mind when I think of our decision to divorce, and it was probably six months after my ex-husband moved out.

We were still going through the divorce process at this point. The papers had been filed, but things weren't finalized yet. It was a weekend afternoon in the fall, just two weeks before Halloween. I decided that I couldn't keep hiding inside, away from the world happening around me, so I made up my mind to take the kids to a pumpkin patch to pick pumpkins. We used to pick pumpkins every year at a nearby farm, as a family unit, ever since the kids had been born. It was that time of year again, which meant time to head to the pumpkin patch for our tradition; this time, minus one. Before this outing, I had avoided many of the activities we used to do as a family. This time, I finally worked up the courage because I knew my kids deserved to keep experiencing life, the activities we used to do, and the traditions we used to have. I knew it was not fair to stop these traditions for them just because I was in my feels.

In the past, we would head to the farm, take a hay ride out to the pumpkin patch, and spend time laughing and giggling as we picked out our pumpkins, which we would later carve. We would then walk around a little bit more, grab some fresh cider, flowers, and veggies from the farmers market, and then head over to a little creamery across the street for some pumpkin ice cream.

This time, as I was being directed to park my car in the field near the farm, I started to get an overwhelming feeling of dread. I began to notice all of these happy families all around me and kept thinking, "How can they be so happy when my world is falling apart?" All of these couples and families were experiencing life together; yet, everything for me was crashing to the ground. As I parked the car, I closed my eyes for a second and reminded myself that I was there for the kids and that I could get through the feelings I would have later when I got home.

That entire day was an absolute struggle for me. Still, I did enjoy so much about that day and the smile on my kids' faces. Another one of my favorite pictures of the boys is from that day; the two of them with their oddly shaped pumpkins in the patch. But it was something that was a struggle to get through. It was hard because we had spent years building this tradition as a family of four, and every happy couple and happy family I saw was a not-so-gentle reminder of my own failure—the failure of my divorce, the failure as a mom, the failure at relationships, and the failure to keep this family unit together. Witnessing other families together reminded me that I was now alone, more alone than ever, even though I had my kids. I found the strength to get through that day by focusing on my gratitude for my kids and concentrating on their laughter and smiles.

Looking back on it, once we got there, everything worked out. We smiled and had a great time, and my kids have wonderful memories from that day because they weren't aware of the internal battle I was facing. I started healing and growing after that, and I no longer feel that way on our traditional outings. I've learned to be grateful that we can still go on these outings, and there's now no arguing, just joy. I had to start focusing on the positives of the situation in order to stop dwelling on the negatives.

Our outings are just the three of us now. We no longer have the tension and arguing that sometimes would ruin these outings; we now have total peace at these outings. I also get to experience my children's full attention; that's something special, something to be cherished.

As we all know, after Halloween and pumpkin picking, Christmas starts to not-so-slowly peek around the corner. The first holiday season that I went through after my divorce was the most challenging holiday season I'd ever experienced. I know that people out there struggle with the holidays because a loved one may have passed around that time, and I imagine that this is what that feels like for them. This holiday season, it was the death of my marriage that I was mourning, the death of a life I had once known.

This holiday was now minus one.

All of the traditions we had built around the holidays would change because some of those traditions were brought into the marriage from his side or were things his family did, and I would no longer be involved in them. This divorce was my opportunity to create new traditions, but it was a struggle to do so that first holiday season after the divorce.

Here, please do something for me. It won't be easy, as your emotional state may still be unstable. Still, I want you to permit yourself to take the time to heal and forgive yourself if you aren't super excited, joyous, and merry during your first holiday season after a divorce. It was especially tough for me my first holiday season because, while I did get to have the kids overnight on Christmas Eve—which was definitely special to me—they left early on Christmas morning right after opening presents to go to their dad's.

I had initially decided that if I couldn't be with my children on Christmas Day, I would do something nice for someone else. So, I planned to do another one of my Divorce Bucket List items, which was taking my grandparents to dinner. Except, I wasn't going to take them out to dinner; I was going to come to their house, surprise them, and cook them a nice Christmas feast. I was then going to stay there to spend time with them, which I hadn't gotten to do much since getting married because of the craziness of raising children and living a few hours away from them.

When my kids left that morning, I started packing up to get ready to head to my grandparents' house when I got a phone call from my mom—who knew what I had been planning. She told me that my grandmother's sister had gone into the hospital, so my grandmother and grandfather would not be home because they were going to see her. I didn't know my grandmother's sister that well, but I did all of the prayers, well-wishes, and family support I could. Once I processed all of that, I realized I was now alone on Christmas Day for the first time ever in my life. Before that year, I had been married or with my family. Now, I was sitting alone on a couch, shocked at the turn of events.

I know a lot of people find themselves alone on Christmas Day, and my heart goes out to them. I'm not trying to whine about it, but everyone's journey and problems are relative to their situation. Personally, this was a hard thing to grasp, especially considering it was the first time for me, and I was still intensely in my feels at this point. I hadn't completed all of my healing yet.

So, I sat there, staring at the wall, wondering how things led me to this moment and why I was being forced to suffer through it alone. I'll never forget the deep sobbing sound I heard next. It was coming out of my body, and it was as if I didn't even recognize myself. I cried as my heart filled with sorrow; it didn't feel right that I couldn't be with my kids on Christmas. I later found out that some people mocked me for a social media post I made about being upset about my time away from my kids. I wish those people well but will never understand how people can be so cold; the only thing I can think of is that they probably needed a hug or compassion more than I did that day.

That Christmas, I must have cried for hours straight, feeling sorry for myself. There were times when I wished I could just fall asleep to wake up the following day and have the pain go away. At some point, one of my neighbors noticed that my car was still around, knowing that I was supposed to be leaving town. I got a call from her asking me what happened. I'm sure she could barely understand what I was saying through my inconsolable crying. Regardless, she invited me over to share Christmas with her family. To this day, I will forever be grateful for that kind gesture because it's the kindness in this world that helps other people get through dark things like divorce, depression, and hopelessness. It's the kind gestures, no matter how small, that help other people. I hope that even if someone doesn't know what it's like to go through a divorce, they can find it in their hearts to not ridicule but give kindness instead to those going through it.

After that first holiday season, I began to find the holidays exciting as a family of three instead of four. We were minus one, but we were building new and exciting traditions. We set our own rules; we have the freedom to do what we want, but the most important thing was the serenity that existed around these holidays. When you're in a toxic relationship, it's very easy for holiday stress to create tension and fighting. While we always did our best not to fight in front of our children when we were married, I am aware that it sometimes happened. Even if the fighting wasn't directly in front of them, children are not dumb; they can sense tension and energy.

It's been a blessing for the kids to experience new holiday memories—memories full of smiles and peace instead of tension. I'm so grateful that even though it was hard to get through that first post-divorce holiday situation, I *was* able to get through it and find peace and joy. I am finally able to be grateful for the positive things on the other side.

Aside from holidays, you may have activities, clubs, hobbies, interests, friends, or specific experiences that you shared together. As you start to walk away from that partnership, you'll realize that many of these things will begin to change and adapt to your new normal.

There are places that you may have gone with your significant other that are hard to face now. You may have shared hobbies, interests, or taken a class together. You may have shared friends.

Now that you're minus one, things do change, but I encourage you not to change yourself; instead, adapt and continue doing the things you love. Do not give up the things you did or places you went to, or the friends you had just because of the discomfort of having that minus one.

There are ways to figure out how to still do the things you love. Maybe you have to change the location of your activity, perhaps you have to get over the discomfort of doing something alone instead of together, but you can do it and still find joy in these activities.

When you go through marriage and start accumulating friends during your marriage, they become what I call mutual marriage friends. It's weird because you don't officially share custody over friends like you do pets or kids, and friends aren't divided up in court like assets. Friendships are often more meaningful than assets, yet it's a taboo part of divorce that isn't often addressed. Someone once told me that while mutual marriage friends don't intentionally choose sides, sometimes it happens naturally.

Unfortunately, I found that I lost a lot of my mutual marriage friends through the divorce process. I wish I could go back and do things differently, as there are many reasons why I lost those friendships. First of all, I was in a dark place at the beginning, and the amount of support I required from friends was astronomical. This burden I imposed is why I suggest spreading out and making new relationships and getting to know people who are going through the same thing as you. That way, you don't overwhelm your friends with the burden of the mass support needed to get through the traumatic divorce experience.

Not only was I highly needy in these relationships, but I also had nothing in my cup to give. I wish I had started my Divorce Bucket List sooner to fill my cup up and start rebuilding earlier than I did so I could have been a better friend to those that were there for me during these dark times.

At the beginning of the divorce, as I was spiraling out of control, I was also self-sabotaging my friendships. If my husband was the person closest to me, knowing everything about me, and he chose to leave me, then why would anyone else stick around? I had let those words he previously told me become something I truly believed; they became my reality. I believed that everyone that I let into my life would leave me because I was a terrible person unworthy of love.

Instead of waiting for these friends to "leave" me like I believed they would, I started to push them away. I regret it. Now that I have learned how to cope and have healed through counseling for my abandonment issues, I mourn the friendships lost due to my self-sabotage.

When you're going through a divorce, there are also other ways you may find that friendships dissipate. It's sadly sometimes just part of the whole traumatic experience. We were super close with some friends, but we'd only really hung out as couples. I found that some of those friendships ended purely out of situational circumstance, just as you may find out. Maybe your ex lives closer to them. Maybe your ex has more in common with them than you. Perhaps some stories are being told to them that aren't true, keeping them away, but remember that you can't control any of those things.

My advice is to not ever focus on the friendships that you're losing. Know that you are worthy, and you are lovable, just the way you are—even at your deepest, darkest experience in life. You bring enough to the table for the people who deserve to be there, around your unique soul. I struggled with focusing on my losses for so long, and I wish I hadn't given so much time, emotion, and distress from my heart to the people who chose not to be around me.

In the end, I know that if they cared enough and false stories were being told to them that they would have asked for my side. I know that if they cared enough and there was a falling out of some sort because of my self-sabotage, we would be able to reconcile—even if years later, down the road. Everyone that's meant to be in your life and stay in your life finds a way. That applies to any type of relationship, romantic or otherwise.

I've also made some beautiful new friendships through my divorce. I've met people who were going through similar things and have connected deeply with them. We've been able to help each other heal and grow, and it's been such a beautiful thing. I'm so grateful for the people I've met through this experience and for the people who stuck around when I was at the lowest point of my life. You can get through these adjustments, but the only way out is through.

PLUS ZERO

I don't even know how the next item on my list came to be. For some reason, I had it in my mind that I wanted to date myself at a wedding. I wanted to be my own wedding date. I wanted to be a "plus zero." So, I wrote on my Divorce Bucket List: "Attend a wedding alone."

It just so happened that I was able to check it off pretty quickly. I was invited to a wedding the fall after creating the list, just seven months after my ex-husband moved out. For some reason, in my mind, going to a wedding alone was a super terrifying thought. I'm a socially extroverted person; I'm not shy, so the fact that it was intimidating for me meant something.

I wanted to go through this wedding experience since the thought of weddings and marriage led to internal anger and resentment because of my divorce, and I wanted to squash that. I wanted to have a positive experience at a wedding and know that marriage and weddings weren't sources of evil—my relationship was just broken.

I needed to prove that to myself.

I knew this would be a delicate situation because the wedding wasn't about me at all. I wanted to make sure my anxieties, beliefs, and resentment would not impact the bride's beautiful day in any way. I also knew I had to face these feelings at some point because I needed to get over my resentment of marriage and weddings to be able to fully be there in support for my friends' future weddings and so that I could heal and move forward.

I knew going into the wedding that I would know only the bride. Leading up to the wedding, there were so many times where I caught myself making excuses. At one point, I almost "called out sick" thinking, "She'll understand, just send her an extra present." I kept trying to find all of these excuses and reasons not to go until I caught myself because, at this point, I had been doing a lot of work trying to heal. I said, "Jenn, this is fear talking." I did a mental exercise that I'll teach you later in this book on the worst-case scenario and realized that the worst case wouldn't harm me and wouldn't have any significant impact on my life. When I realized that, I became steadfast in my decision to attend and to do so alone.

I created a plan just in case my worst-case scenario of feeling extremely awkward did happen—I know, not that bad of a worst-case, is it? I decided that if I felt unbearably uncomfortable or overly awkward at any point because of being alone at this wedding, I would simply hide in the bathroom on my phone. When I went to this wedding, I made sure that my phone was fully charged—just in case I needed to use this backup plan.

The ceremony was lovely. The reception was a buffet without assigned seating which was terrifying for me. As I walked into the romantically lit barn room where the reception was being held, the first thing I thought was, "Where am I going to sit?" It was one of those things where, in my head, I just imagined walking up to all these tables only to hear, "You can't sit with us." That thought was absolutely irrational. Do you know how friendly people can be in most cases? I mean, especially if you're willing to smile. That's it; a smile was all it took to be accepted at a table.

I walked up to the first table I found with an empty seat, smiled at them, and simply said, "I'm solo tonight, and I don't know anybody. Do you mind if I sit here?" Holy crap, did I feel awkward, but they welcomed me into their table with open arms. I was grateful at the time that I had food in front of me because when you have food to focus on, you don't have to talk too much.

Food only lasts so long, though. Once I was done eating, it was time to face the scary part of socializing with people I didn't know. After dinner, the DJ was going strong, and the dance floor started filling up. You are probably expecting me to tell you this inspirational story about how I summoned the courage to head out to the dance floor and danced my way into some type of awakening. I'm not good at lying, so I'm just going to be honest—I stayed at that table almost the whole time!

I found that it was easier than I thought to make friends with the people I was sitting with. A couple of times, the people from the table would go do their thing, and I would be left at the table by myself, staring at the wall. I remember feeling super awkward when these moments would happen, but they wouldn't last much longer than five minutes, even though they felt like hours.

I did decide, finally, during one of those awkward moments, to get up and try to meet new people. It was so scary to walk up to a group of people who I'd never talked to before, but I did. I introduced myself, my heart beating through my ears. I ended up hanging out with a friendly group of couples around my age for the rest of the night. I survived being alone at the wedding and even found myself smiling from time to time. More importantly, it was a freeing experience.

I woke up the next day feeling brand new. I was rejuvenated. Experiencing the celebration of someone else's love didn't cause negative emotions like I thought it would. I was purely happy for them. The ceremony and experience gave me hope. I found that I could believe in things like love, marriage, and weddings again and know that I would be okay on my own, no matter what ... minus one or plus zero, no matter what, I would be okay on my own.

When I realized I could be okay on my own, I started finding my confidence again and felt alive again. Before that, I had felt like a zombie in a daze going through my divorce. As I began to step into this new confidence, I started to feel energetic again. I began to live my life instead of just going through the motions. Going to the wedding helped me begin to love the idea of love again. And that's genuinely what I wish for everyone who's going through a divorce. So, now, I challenge you to add something to your Divorce Bucket List that centers around getting uncomfortable on your own, without anyone around to lean on—whatever that might look like for you.

DATE YOURSELF CHALLENGE

Pick a night in the next ten days when you can treat yourself to a date, completely alone. It doesn't have to be fancy or expensive. Simply challenge yourself to get out and do something you really enjoy. Date yourself! The more you get a little bit uncomfortable, the more you will start feeling empowered and confident in this new life!

Step 1- Pick a date and time – write "SOLO DATE" in your planner or virtual calendar or set an alarm reminder on your phone.

Step 2- Pick an activity – it could be something you used to do that brought you joy, something you like doing now but haven't in a bit, or even something you do now but generally with other people.

Step 3- Make any appointment/reservation as needed, depending on the activity you choose.

Step 4- ENJOY! Then, when you get home, take some time to reflect—How did you feel? What was your favorite part? Was it as scary as you expected it to be? Will you do it again? What could you try next time to bring yourself more joy and confidence?

Learning To Share

I know that not everyone going through a divorce has kids, but if you do, I hope this helps you. If not, feel free to read for entertainment or skip ahead to the next chapter!

Sharing The Blues

I mentioned before how I used to cry every time my boys left to go to their dad's house. For an entire year, every time they left, I cried. I'm not talking about shedding a tear; I'm talking full-on sobbed with my back against the door right after I closed it, curled up with my face in my knees. I would spend the entire night on my couch with a stomachache, thinking, "This is so not fair for them. I've failed them as a mother; this isn't natural, it's not how it's supposed to be."

Quiet time can become quite scary after the typical hustle and bustle of married life with children around 24/7. It's like having an empty nest way before you expect one. At first, the quiet time can seem depressing, but you can train yourself to enjoy the time to yourself after a while.

Slowly, the crying lasted less and less time. As even more time passed, I've learned that it's okay not to have things be "how they were planned/supposed to be" because there are things to be admired about the unusual.

This unusual, unexpected, new dynamic that my kids and I have has left us with so many gifts. I now love that every second I spend with them is completely cherished, even the tough days. When they are not with me, I focus on the blessing that I have the time to refresh, think, and grow as a person and plan fun things for us to do together when they are back.

One day, after an entire year of drowning in my sorrow and pain, for the very first time, when they left, I didn't cry; I smiled. They get to spend quality time with both of us in positive atmospheres, and while it was extremely tough to decide, go through, and adjust to, I am content and at peace with where we are.

I want anyone who is going through something heavy to know that there is always peace somewhere later through the journey, so here are the things I found helpful to cope with what I referred to as my shared custody blues and find happiness in this new normal.

Fill Your Calendar – Take small steps to start scheduling things ahead of time for when your kids will not be with you. Call up friends you have lost touch with—because we all know that happens when we get married—and set up a coffee or wine date! Schedule trips with your friends or family for the weekends you don't have the kids. You don't necessarily have to be dating someone new to fill your calendar up with fun dates and distract yourself from your emotions.

Practice New Self-Care Habits –Develop some new habits to improve and grow yourself. I started taking a candlelit bath with a book and a glass of wine every night my kids left for their week with Dad—yeah, I know, super cliché— but it became this little routine that helped me de-stress from the single mom week and transition into a calm and happy place with myself. You can practice meditation, read books, do skin care, whatever it is that makes YOU happy. Start getting into the routine of showing yourself a little love during your downtime.

Develop a New Skill – One of the best ways to lift your spirits is to improve your confidence. And trust me, I know that when you are in the midst of a major life change—aka divorce—it is super hard to feel confident about literally anything. Learning a new skill helps to improve your confidence, whether you are looking for it or not! Try to use your spare time to take a class, pick up a new hobby, pick up an old one you left behind when you had kids, or finally pursue something you were always curious about.

SHARING THE BURDENS AND BLISS

For me, one of the scariest parts of the divorce was the fear of how it would impact the kids. Even though I didn't know exactly what going through the divorce would look like for any of us, I knew that it would be extremely difficult and that nobody would come out the same person they were when we entered into it. I'm thankful we were required to attend a co-parenting class when we went to court for custody because that class brought up some constructive advice that I may not have thought of on my own. They pointed out little things that I could now be self-aware of and control my actions around to make the transition as easy as possible for the kids.

I do have to say that, while I went through a chaotic journey internally, the one thing I think we did best—so far—throughout the separation, divorce, and beyond was minimizing the impact on our kids. They were thrown through a loop with change after change because of the divorce, but they are utterly thriving now. I believe that they are doing so well because, for our family, they were our number one priority through everything. My mindset after taking that co-parenting class became: Mad at the ex-spouse? Doesn't matter; deal with it later—kids first. Hurting? You can cry into your pillow later—kids first. Here are some tips on the things that I believe we did "right" in hopes that it may help you consciously do your best co-parenting through this crazy experience.

My Co-Parenting Tips

- We immediately set up communication boundaries. My ex-husband started this by creating an "email only" rule when we started the divorce process. I remember being so annoyed with him for not responding to calls or texts at first, thinking it was silly and childish. In hindsight, I think it was best for us to have these boundaries because it taught us how to communicate with fewer emotions. It's easy to have an emotional response via calls/texts, but emails forced us to step back, analyze our priorities, and think through what was best for the children. Now that time has passed, and emotions have settled, we've gotten to the point where we can now do the same over calls and texts.

- We made it a non-negotiable rule to never talk about the other parent in front of the children. If we were mad or upset and needed to vent to someone, we would do whatever it took to control our emotions until we could step away from the kids and call a family member or friend to talk where the kids could not hear us.

- As soon as we got an agreed—or court-ordered—custody schedule in place, we got organized. We use the app "Cozi," which manages our schedules, but many options exist. There are even apps where you can communicate in-app only to help with the communication boundaries, too!

- Flexibility became crucial. Emotions run high during divorce, but that doesn't mean life stops. Sometimes things change, and you have to adapt to those changes. We decided to be flexible and fair with each other. If plans changed, we did our best to help each other out; after all, who doesn't want more time with their kids!? Before COVID, we were doing a 2-2-3-3 type of schedule. Once COVID hit, we were basically forced to change our schedule to week on, week off, something we had initially both ultimately vetoed at the beginning of the process. We made the change because it made sense with transfers back and forth during a pandemic but found out that this new schedule worked better for everyone!

- Our kids were old enough to understand a bit of what was going on, so we kept constant lines of communication open with them. There were many times where I would just ask my kids, individually, "How are you doing?", "What could I be doing to make this easier for you?" or "What's on your mind?" And then I would just listen.

- Expectations were set going into it. I knew there would be conflict, but the more I worked on myself, improving my mindset and healing, the easier it was for me to deal with the conflict calmly. Once I let go of things I could not control (like my ex-husband taking my son against my wishes to a shooting range), I was able to focus on things I could control (like educating my son on safety). The more I did my routines and affirmations, the more I was able to train my mind to problem-solve instead of emotionally react. It's a much happier and peaceful place to be, and the kids don't have to deal with the emotional fallout either.

Adjusting to co-parenting can be challenging, but it doesn't have to break you—or the kids. Remember to cut yourself some slack as you all adapt to the new situation. Then, use the tips above to step into being the best version you can be as a co-parent, single parent, or whatever type of parent your situation calls for.

It's a Marathon

Back in middle school, I had a tech-ed teacher; he was one of those "cool" teachers that you could actually talk to, and he was a mentor of sorts. I grew up in the countryside where a farm was behind and in front of our house. I remember seeing my tech-ed teacher—who was also the cross-country coach—run past my childhood house during my school years. I knew he lived in town, so him being near my home had to mean he had been running for miles. I remember thinking that he was absolutely insane.

I was always pretty athletic growing up. I was in softball, basketball, field hockey, dance, cheerleading, and volleyball, just to name a few. It shouldn't come as a surprise, then, that I enjoy running. I'm that person that people look out of their window at and ask, "Ewwww, why is she running? Is someone chasing her?" I have been into running since I was in the sixth grade, mostly thanks to field hockey. Although I enjoy running, I had never run competitively in track or cross-country, and I had never run a race, not even a 5K, by the time my divorce started.

My best friend growing up, Karen, was always super into running, and that's one of the things we bonded over through the years. For some reason, every time she asked me to do a race with her, I let my fear overcome me. It's not like I wasn't already running three to five miles a day the first time she asked me to run a 5K with her. I just didn't know what it would be like. I was afraid of the possibility that I would be having a bad running day and fail at it. I was scared I wouldn't be able to train enough for it. So, I always turned her down. I remember when she ran her first half-marathon, though. I was so proud of her and in complete awe. I was surprised to find myself a tad jealous when she did it, but I caught myself. How dare I feel jealous! She asked me to run with her, and I let my fear talk me out of it. I lectured myself for not doing it with her and then went ahead and ran five miles the next day as part of my regular routine.

When I made my Divorce Bucket List, I knew that a lot of the things I was going to put on it would have to do with facing fears. It was exciting and terrifying at the same time when I wrote the words "Run A 5K" on my list. It wasn't one of the first things I wrote, but I spent a lot of time thinking about ways to improve my confidence and self-love again, and I knew that completing something that had always scared me would do just that.

When I was finally ready to tackle this item on the list, I decided the best way to do it would be via Disney. You've probably already gotten the message here, but just in case: I live and breathe Disney. I swear if I have one regret in life, it's that I didn't do something that led to a career there. It's not just the fairy tale of it all; I am beyond mesmerized with the business genius of Walt Disney, with his drive and passion, and with the operations of the entire company. It's just a bonus that everything Disney speaks to my inner princess, right? The only obvious way to approach running a race would be to run one during the Disney Princess Marathon Weekend.

At this point, I hadn't been running more than maybe two miles a week because of the depression from the divorce mixed with adapting to single mom life. I decided I wanted to run my first race with someone on the same page as me, and I texted my friend, Ann, who I knew loved Disney just as much as I did and had recently started running herself.

"Want to run the Disney Princess 5K with me?" I asked.

"I just looked. It's sold out. The half-marathon is open-should we? lol," she texted back.

During the previous year, neither of us had run more than two miles at one time, which leads me to believe that it was my Must-Do Mindset talking when I replied, "Okay, let's do the damn half!" That afternoon, we both hit the register button and signed up to run 13.1 miles in Disney the following February.

We registered at the end of July, which gave us about seven months to train, so I knew that if I were disciplined and focused, I would be able to do it. I could really use the distraction, after all.

Participating in a Run Disney event is unlike anything I have ever experienced before in my life, and it was one of the neatest things that I've ever done in my life to date. In true Disney fashion, they leave no detail unturned. Every step of the way is a literal piece of magic.

Knowing that I would be running at Disney helped keep me motivated to train, but I did not train like an actual full-on marathon runner. I trained as a single mom of two who worked sixty hours—or more—a week and did it as she found time.

I remember the excitement in the days leading up to the event. I was so nervous but also so enthusiastic. I was concerned that I wouldn't finish it because you had to complete the half-marathon at a certain pace not to get kicked off the course. To me, finishing this half-marathon was symbolic of overcoming the obstacles in my life that I was experiencing—like self-doubt, fear, and insecurities, all of which stemmed from the divorce.

Ann and I arrived at our resort the day before the run. As we walked into the Polynesian, we were immediately surrounded by the all-encompassing Disney feels; there was just nothing but pure excitement remaining as the nervousness completely left my body.

On the day of the run, we got up at 2:30 in the morning, which sounds crazy when you think about it. We were getting up at 2:30 in the morning and then running 13.1 miles afterward. It turns out, when you do a Disney half-marathon, you end up doing so much walking to get to and from the race itself that you likely cover at least seventeen miles that day. Add in going to the parks afterward, as we did, and I think we surpassed twenty-five miles for the entire day. I don't think I've ever moved my legs so much in one day in my life!

Before arriving, I created a playlist and filled it with pumped-up songs, including, of course, some of my Disney favorites. I made sure the playlist was over three hours long. It was mainly to keep myself distracted while running. I also got some great advice to dedicate each of my thirteen miles to something meaningful to me. I thought this idea was perfect, considering the whole race was self-dedicated to overcoming the tribulations of divorce and rediscovering myself. Finishing this race would prove to myself that I am strong, powerful, and capable of achieving crazy things that I never thought I could, just like I didn't believe I could run this race and just like I didn't think I could go through a divorce and come out happy on the other side. But look, I've done both. I took the advice and drilled down further, dedicating each mile to someone or something important in my life.

Here is what I dedicated each of my thirteen full miles to for that run:

- Mile 1 – My brother, Josh
- Mile 2 – The future success of my business
- Mile 3 – Leaving the past behind me
- Mile 4 – Pappy's health
- Mile 5 – Nanny's health
- Mile 6 – My children
- Mile 7 – Pappy Gus – I miss him still
- Mile 8 – Grandma – I'll never forget her impact on my life
- Mile 9 – Dad's health and insight
- Mile 10 – Mom's health and insight
- Mile 11 – My other little brother that passed away
- Mile 12 – Loving myself where I'm at
- Mile 13 – The future

Arriving at the race, I thought I would have some sort of dread, fear, or even desire to run—away from the race. I didn't! I felt nothing but pure excitement and determination. I had done everything I could think of to prepare myself, and I was ready to face this challenge.

Waiting for the race to start was truly a magical time. Runners were split into multiple "corrals" based on past times or projected finish times. I was in corral G since I was a new racer and got to witness the excitement for about an hour and a half of watching the other corrals start their race. As each corral lined up to start, there were fireworks, songs, and so much excitement. I met some fantastic people in my corral who I still keep in touch with to this day. In fact, two of us ended up going through divorces and leaning on each other from time to time. I took so much more than I expected away from that race.

As it was my corral's turn, I braced myself for what I knew would be an incredible journey into the unknown. I had read a lot ahead of time but knew I wouldn't truly understand what it was like until I experienced it. As the corral G fireworks lit the sky, I began my run. The first few miles were so simple; it's really easy to keep yourself going forward when everyone around you is doing the same. Everyone ran at different paces but were all still moving forward—together.

There was one singular moment of the race that defined the entire experience for me. I even have the painful kind of goosebumps happening right now as I write this. As you're running, they have mile markers; each has the mile on it and a Disney character, so you can stop and take a quick picture if you want. At this point, I had turned the corner to start running down Main Street in Magic Kingdom, the sight of Cinderella's Castle just coming into my view. As I got closer to the castle, I was already beginning to feel tears in my eyes. It was such a meaningful moment. The mile marker was right in front of the castle, and it was the peak moment that most people look forward to when doing this run.

Running towards the castle, I made a mental note to get into the present moment purposefully. I wanted to notice everything around me—all of the feelings, sounds, and sights— and be able to look back and truly cherish the details of the moment.

I had turned off my playlist when I first entered Magic Kingdom because I noticed they had Disney music playing throughout the park for all to hear. As the castle and the mile marker grew closer and closer, I noticed something magical. The song "A Whole New World" was playing over the speakers.[1] The song's lyrics were telling me that, similar to a shooting star, I had come too far to return to where I came from. The timing couldn't have been more perfect, hearing those exact words right at that moment.

At that moment, as I was running, tears began streaming down my face. I heard the message and agreed. I *had* come so far, and no, I *could not* go back to where I used to be. Not in the race and not in my life. I knew I was achieving what I had set out to achieve. It didn't even matter what time I finished the race that day. Whether referring to the run or my life, I was going to do new things, and I was going to pursue my desires.

Hearing that song, I heard a message, whoever it was from, loud and clear: "Jenn, your life is just beginning. You are finding yourself and becoming a better person. You were afraid to step away from your marriage, but new horizons are waiting. There are hard things that are going on in your life, but that's nothing compared to what you can achieve, what you're born to achieve, and what you're going to achieve."

I continued the race and met some fun people along the way. By mile eight, I thought my legs were going to fall off completely. At mile eleven, I found a second wind and knew I could get it done.

As I crossed the finish line—my legs barely moving—I nearly collapsed with my sense of accomplishment. I cried for the second time that race, this time out of something I didn't even know I possessed. I was finally proud of myself. I don't think I've ever experienced the sense of self-pride that accompanied those tears in my life, prior to or since that race.

I instantly felt like I was Superwoman; I could do anything! If I could run 13.1 miles, then I was capable of doing other things I thought impossible. I was going to make sure this divorce did not ruin me. I know that not everyone is into running. I know that not everyone is into exercise, but I encourage you to find something that challenges you, that you don't think you can do, that has always kind of been in the back of your head, that you've thought about doing, and put that on your list. Then put down this book and take action to sign up for it or make the first step toward it. It's going to be scary. You're going to think it's impossible, but when you achieve it, you're going to feel so much empowerment within yourself. It's going to change everything for you.

Race Running Hacks

- Download a training app—I used the app "13.1" — with a training schedule you can realistically follow. Using the plan within the app, map your runs into whatever calendar you use, ex. iCal, a planner, monthly wall calendar, etc. By combining the app's helpful training plan with your written-down commitment in your calendar, you are more likely to stick to the schedule.
- As I mentioned above, another thing I did that helped me through the overwhelming length of the race was dedicating my miles to someone or something. Doing this held me accountable and motivated me to stay strong, even during the most challenging miles when my legs started to protest. It was also a great distraction.
- Try to pick a race that aligns with something you care about. There are so many different fun runs and themed races that you can choose from. It helps when you find one that has some meaning to you, whether it's a certain fun theme or a cause you are supporting. Relating to the run is excellent motivation to train for and complete it.
- Invest in great running shoes! My quality shoes made such a difference for me when it came to training and running.
- Running buddies definitely help keep you accountable! I even enlisted my oldest son to run some of my shorter training runs with me. It turned out he loved running

too, and he ended up joining the cross-country team at his school!
- On race day, enjoy every single second of your run. You will feel so great when you cross that finish line, so take everything in and fully allow yourself to experience it all!
- Use Google! I cannot tell you how many running blogs I read leading up to the race. They gave great advice on running gear, nutrition, etc.
- Gear I used and wouldn't race without- a running belt, arm phone holder, headphones, Vaseline on my toes before the run, Brooks running shoes, Guu—strawberry banana is my fav, a running playlist, and my Apple Watch—to track progress between markers. I keep it pretty basic and have had an unbelievable time each time I've raced, completing several races since that first half-marathon.

Reminder – You can do hard things!

Progress, Not Perfection (Yet)

I've always prided myself on the ability to own my mistakes. Throughout my marriage, I made a lot of them. The problem with my marriage was that we just kept making mistakes together and hurting each other. It got to a point where the toxicity level was so high that there was no recovering from it.

We had gotten married at such a young age, both having our own issues that we brought into the marriage, and instead of approaching these issues together, we came it as him versus me and me versus him. Things only got worse from there as we dealt with over a decade of life's ups and downs, traumas, experiences, and devastations that were thrown our way.

I wanted to share a couple of my mistakes throughout the divorce process that I wish people had given me a heads-up about. I want to share them with you so you don't make the same mistakes.

The first mistake I made was that I was so terrified, I became frozen in place. I would not leave my bed for days. I was in denial. I did not take action. I know that when you're going through a divorce, sometimes it's much easier to cry into a bottle of wine—or three—and sleep until noon than it is to get up and go after what you want. If I could do it again, I would give myself a few days that I needed to cope. Then I would take immediate steps to defrost, start taking action and start moving forward again.

I would also get a support system around me as soon as possible to help me take the actions I needed to start going after what I desired. There were points in the divorce process where I could have been more proactive. There were things like custody issues based on past circumstances that I could have fought harder for. There were issues around money and my right to the money I made, which I could have fought harder for. There were also things like putting a structure in place for the kids to take some of the emotional burdens off them that I could have fought harder for in the beginning.

In the beginning, instead of getting up and taking action and fighting for what I deserved, I focused so much effort on things that didn't matter. It was like I was going through something so traumatic that, instead of dealing with the actual traumatic event, I started creating new but slightly less traumatic events to go through. Remember the whole rebound and how I broke my own heart with that? It was easier to create a heartbreak situation that didn't even exist and to deal with that pain than it was to deal with the pain coming from the complete upheaval of my entire life and mourning the loss of what my life was supposed to be.

I do encourage anyone reading this to take the time to give yourself room to mourn—to be sad. Divorce is a death, as in it's a death of the life you built. If you are going through a divorce, you are dealing with some pretty heavy shit! You will need to process your emotions to cope before you fully feel ready to rebuild. Just don't stop taking action—no matter how small— while you're mourning and learning to cope.

The easiest way to keep yourself moving forward is to get a support system in place as soon as possible; that support system can look like anything. It can be friends, family, counselors, coaches, or groups—this support system should hold you accountable while also providing emotional support. Don't put off that meeting to get yourself a lawyer. Don't put off getting all of your documents in order. Don't put off filing for a divorce if that's what you want. Don't put off what you could do today until tomorrow just because of your emotional upheaval.

Yes, easier said than done, but I promise you that if you can get one or two people in your corner to cheer you on and help spur you into action, it will assist you significantly. For me, that came in the form of a life coach, but for you, it might be a friend, coach, or counselor. Once I finally let that mentor in, I was able to start taking action.

Another mistake I made was my approach to obtaining legal counsel. I did some research and had my heart set on a specific lawyer. I called to set up my initial meeting with that lawyer, having no other option in mind. Her office called me back to let me know that my husband had already retained her. If I had acted quicker, I would have had the lawyer I wanted. From there, I felt an initial defeat before the process even started. Ironically, that lawyer and my now ex-husband terminated that relationship, and he ended up having completely different counsel by the time we got to our proceedings.

It's essential to set expectations to keep your options open when it comes to hiring your divorce team because things you don't expect to happen will occur, and, usually, they happen for a reason. The lawyer who I ended up hiring was referred to me by a friend. I absolutely adored my lawyer's practice and skills, and he really worked well in my favor. I was not, however, prepared for the fact that during the divorce, you may have one, two, three, or more lawyers throughout the entire experience, so be prepared.

When I got the phone call from my lawyer that afternoon, I thought he was just calling to give me an update on our court dates. I was shocked to hear him say, "Jenn, I just wanted to let you know, I'm fed up with family law. I don't want to do it anymore, so I am changing practices." He had decided to quit family law to practice law in, let's just call it, the "grass" industry. This news was devastating for me because I had found a lawyer I worked well with; he was a great advocate for me, and I didn't know if I would trust anyone else to do as good of a job as he did.

I froze again. After I talked to some people who had gone through the same thing, I found out it's not uncommon to have more than one lawyer throughout the process. I urge everyone to have backups in place for legal counsel—if you choose to hire a lawyer. Had somebody told me that it was possible that the lawyer in the beginning would probably not be the lawyer at the end, I think I'd have been a little bit more prepared, both with documenting everything as well as having a backup lawyer in mind.

My next lawyer taught me some lessons as well. I hired her after our initial meeting because she was a bulldog; I loved her vibe, her energy, and she seemed very intelligent. At our consult, it felt like we "clicked." Based on what she told me, I knew I found a new partner advocating for what I desired. She told me the things we were going to do to get where I wanted to be. I seriously thought, "Wow, why was I afraid? This woman seems even better than the last guy I had."

Now, keep this in mind: You go into meetings with these lawyers, and you often have to pay a decent fee even to have the initial appointment to see if you want to hire them. Then, if you decide you like them, you pay a more significant retainer fee.

Little did I know that a few days after paying my retainer, my new lawyer would transfer me to her partner without asking my opinion on it. Then I would have to pay to fill the new partner in on everything I'd already paid to tell the first partner I had met with!

I tell this story so others can be prepared for that. While sometimes our emotions are high and we want to be mad, we can't fault these lawyers on it because they're just trying to make a living, and holding a grudge or getting angry is not going to help at all. Instead, we can focus on things we can control, and if you know that these things could potentially happen, you can prepare. Prepare with documentation. A lack of preparation is a massive mistake for divorce; it could cost you a lot of money. This advice also relates back to the point of not allowing yourself to freeze—take action.

Start preparing by fully documenting all of your information. The more organized you are, the less you're going to pay. If I had documented everything from my conversation with my second lawyer before she passed me off to her partner, then I wouldn't have spent a couple hundred per hour to fill the partner in. I could have paid less to send an email with everything thoroughly documented and organized. I encourage you to take a couple of minutes and put this book down, get a notebook, write an email to yourself, or save it in a Word document—whatever feels best to you. Write some bullet points of the important things related to your marriage and divorce. Here are just some things to consider documenting:

- Key events and turning points in your marriage
- Key events in your separation
- Key events in your divorce proceedings
- What are your main concerns about the divorce?
- What are your goals for custody/assets/financials?
- Document important dates
- Document current financial and asset information
- Document current debt information
- Document information about your children
- Get a list of relevant documents and save them in an accessible location (i.e., taxes, bank statements, credit card statements, any previous court paperwork for the divorce- including the filing, mortgage information, etc.)

Being organized will help you stay prepared for any changes you may have in your legal team.

Keep in mind, as well, that there are times you'll find yourself becoming emotionally exhausted as you're going through the divorce process. I became emotionally exhausted very quickly during my journey because I hadn't started working on my Divorce Bucket List yet. I hadn't started working on myself, my goals, dreams, and desires, and I hadn't begun helping myself move forward. I was stuck in that dark place, feeling afraid and full of emotions. Because of this, I didn't fight as hard for things that I wanted.

We had a pup, Goose—a gorgeous chocolate lab we had adopted as a family of four— who initially stayed in the marital residence with me when my ex-husband first moved out.

We had adopted Goose from a coworker's brother, who had to get rid of him. Poor Goose had failed out of retrieving school, so his first owner gave him away because he didn't want to deal with him as a pet. My coworker's brother adopted him but soon found out that his wife was not interested in keeping him, so he had to rehome him. So, after a family meeting, we decided we would welcome Goose into our family and his fur-ever home.

The only problem was that Goose was living in Georgia, and we were in Pennsylvania.

We found a website where you can hire people to drive things to you. I'm not talking about Uber or DoorDash; you can literally have someone bring a couch from Florida to Texas or a dog from

Georgia to Pennsylvania. So, we hired someone to drive Goose to us.

It took the driver a few days longer than expected to finally arrive. We were all so excited when we welcomed him into our family. He was a seven-month-old puppy at the time. Being a lab, he was pretty big for a puppy, but he still had that puppy energy and the big lab puppy tail. When a lab has that puppy energy, but they've grown big, they're pretty reckless. It was an interesting couple of years as he grew out of his puppy mode and started to realize how big he was. Regardless, we all fell absolutely in love with this dog.

Fast forward to about two and a half months after my ex-husband moved out. On this particular weekend, I had to leave town for a speaking engagement. My kids were coming with me because it was near my parents' house so they could hang out with them. I asked my now ex-husband to go to the house, let Goose out, and feed him while I was gone. When I came home from the event, I noticed that Goose was not there, and neither was his cage, food, bowls, or toys ... all gone. I was devastated because, up until that point, Goose had stayed with me; he was my running buddy and offered me companionship and security.

I was so upset at the loss of a pet; it was similar to the death of a pet. I cry as I write this because I know I simply didn't fight hard enough for Goose—sometimes I wonder if he thought I didn't love him when he didn't see me for almost a year after that day. I should have fought harder since he was like a child, but, to me, having him taken like that was a blow on top of many blows throughout the divorce negotiations. I was emotionally exhausted.

In the years leading up to my rebuilding, I learned that we can handle so much more than we think. So, don't give up when something comes your way in your divorce that you think you can't take. If you genuinely want that thing, fight for it. Fight even if you are tired.

In hindsight, I do wish I had fought for partial custody of Goose, at least for a little bit of time, while we all adjusted to the situation. As I write this, he's still living with my ex, and he's happy there. Now that emotions are more settled, I get to see him every once in a while, so things are okay. Still, I do wish, at least for some time, that we had shared partial custody of Goose. I wish I had fought for what he deserved, what I deserved, and what I had the rights to.

Not assessing your new family budget is another really easy mistake to make. I made it myself, which was surprising to many people since I have a finance degree. Divorce is overwhelming; it's easy to overlook things and make mistakes. I know a lot of you might be reading this book and thinking, "Well, of course, she could do all of these Divorce Bucket List activities. She was self-employed and financially set." That is the furthest thing from the truth; the financial aspect of my divorce was the scariest part—next to custody. My husband decided to leave less than a year after we agreed on me leaving my six-figure guaranteed salary job to pursue my dream of being self-employed. Being self-employed is not always easy—there are great things about it, but there are also expenses to build and substantial investments to make in the beginning. While my business was doing well in revenue when we started the divorce, it was not profitable enough to fund a single-income household.

I was running a successful business, but that business also had expenses that needed to be paid, so I felt the same impact as many of those going from a two-income household to a one-income household with full family expenses. I was absolutely terrified. I don't want to give financial advice in this book (maybe in a future one), but I want you to know that if I could do it, you can do it, too. It's super overwhelming in the beginning, but there are so many options and so many ways you can improve your financial situation, despite the loss in household income.

My advice is to start with my Divorce Budget Planning Worksheet; it is how I started to get over the overwhelming idea of a single-income household and figure out where I needed to make changes to tackle the new budget. I then cut out my limiting beliefs and started using that Must-Do Mindset to make things work. You can download your free [Divorce Budget Planning Worksheet](go.divideguide.com/budget) here:

go.divideguide.com/budget

Several other things happened that I wish I had fought for, but, at the time, I was just too weak. We can't afford to be helpless in our divorces. We are our only heroes. You are the one soldier in your individual army. We do not have time to be weak when fighting for what we deserve and what we have the right to. We can have vulnerable moments where we can cry into a pillow because we're hurting. We can even scream into that pillow. But then we have to get back up and fight because if we don't get back up and fight, nobody will do it for us. The lawyer is not going to fight any harder than you want to fight. Your counselors and coaches aren't going to fight any harder than you're willing to fight beside them. You are ultimately responsible for being the one who gets up and fights for everything you want and deserve through your divorce. It becomes even more important that you fight for rebuilding through and after your divorce because you are the only person responsible for rebuilding that new life.

Yes, there was a life you dreamed and envisioned as your permanent happily ever after. It's being re-written—now your happily ever after is evolving, and you get to rewrite the story. The chapter of your marriage may have come to an end, much like the current chapter of this book is about to end. The great thing is, you're about to turn the page. While you might not have a say in what happens in the next chapter of this book, you have ultimate control over the next and rest of the chapters you're writing about your life, through your divorce, and beyond. You get to create a new meaning of *your* happily ever after.

Old, New, Borrowed, Blue

Something Old

When you're going through a divorce, old relationships can change, and mine changed a lot. As I mentioned before, I lost a lot of friends. Regardless of how hard you try, it's inevitable that sometimes these relationships change. Family relationships will inevitably change as well.

One of the hardest things for me through my divorce was the change in my relationship with my in-laws. My sister-in-law was one of my best friends ever in this entire lifetime. I'll always view her as my sister. Matter-of-fact, there were times where it felt like she was more like my sister than my ex-husband's sister; we had grown that close. We shared so much together, and I loved every second I spent with her.

On a rainy June day, shortly after my ex-husband moved out, I decided it was time for some new ink. I already had a few tattoos, but they were all smaller in size. I had added "finally get your thigh tattoo" to my Divorce Bucket List. I didn't have an appointment that day but got lucky when I walked in because they had a cancellation. During the six-hour-long session, I texted my sister-in-law and asked if she wanted to meet up for dinner afterward. She said yes. Up to this point, we had been pretty inseparable, like real sisters. She met me at the tattoo parlor just as we were finishing up, and I showed off the two black roses now adorning my entire upper thigh—symbolic of love gained, love lost, and passion. I chose two roses to symbolize my two sons, the most amazing gift I was taking away from the marriage and symbolizing my love for them that could never end.

As we sat down to dinner, I wanted so much for everything just to remain the way it was between us leading up to the divorce. I did think, for some reason, that maybe we could defy odds and keep the sisterly bond that we had and stay as close as we were. Unfortunately, in the end, that didn't happen. As we were waiting for our meals to come, my sister-in-law started crying. She told me she didn't want to lose me. I cried with her as I promised her that we wouldn't lose each other and that this divorce wouldn't impact us, but I think we both knew deep down that things could never be the same.

To this day, I still love her as my sister, and I always will. We still get together sometimes; it's just not the close relationship it used to be because of the divorce. I am sure it has to be a complicated situation for her, so I respect that.

When you're going through a divorce, just be aware that relationships are fluid and constantly evolving. Some relationships may change multiple times while you're going through the divorce.

You never know what might happen a year, two years, five years down the road. It's possible that people may reconnect and come back into your life when things aren't as rocky, and emotions are more settled. Find comfort in that.

Another in-law of mine whom I was really close with was my mother-in-law. She's always been easy to talk to. I leaned on her at various times throughout my marriage—learning a lot from her along the way. Because of our open communication and shared interests, we became very close. We went through some crazy ups and downs together, and things like that tend to bring you even closer.

At the start of the divorce, we went out to lunch, and both cried over soup, reaffirming to each other that we would always maintain the love and respect we had, no matter what happened, and we kept to that. We aren't as close anymore because it's difficult to remain close with an ex-in-law, but we are still very respectful and have hearts full of love for each other.

I had a conversation with her one day during my son's sporting event when she shared something with me that someone had once taught her. I thought it was so relevant and accurate that I have to share it with you now. Going through life is a lot like driving a car down the road. As you're driving, you have a windshield, the largest window in the car, but you also have a rearview mirror. The rearview mirror is much smaller than the windshield. Even though it's smaller, the rearview mirror is still an essential aspect of driving regarding your safety and the safety of those around you.

In life, it's rather easy for us to focus on the things in the rearview mirror—the past. As we're going through a divorce, it's easy to focus on what that person did to us, no matter how two-way of a street it may have been. It's easy to focus on the negative and what happened in the past that caused us to feel certain feelings. It's easy to stare into that rearview mirror, obsessing over acts of the past that led to the divorce. But when we do that, we miss the view in the windshield: the largest window in the car.

The windshield shows us where we're going. If we're not watching where we're headed, then we're going to crash. It's crucial when you're going through a divorce to not only focus on the things that happened but pay attention to where you're going, and focus on rebuilding, regrowing, and getting to a point where you are yourself again.

You do this by concentrating on the windshield, keeping focused on where you're going, and only occasionally glancing into that rearview mirror for safety. You're going to glance into that rearview mirror to remind yourself of mistakes, things you do and don't want, and lessons that you've learned from the experiences you've been through. But after looking into that rearview mirror to briefly remind yourself of these things, you need to go right back to focusing out that larger windshield because that's showing what is ahead.

It's time to focus on you; it's time to focus on your goals; it's time to rebuild.

After I had that conversation with her, it became so clear to me that my Divorce Bucket List was exactly what needed to be my priority in my life. I needed to focus on these goals, desires, and dreams for myself, my kids, and my future. I wouldn't be able to move past my divorce and rebuild and regrow if I didn't start focusing on the future.

As I was going through these changing relationships, I realized that a lot of what was happening to me wasn't as scary as I thought it would be. Again, proving our fears are often more frightening than the actual situation—we always assume that worst-case scenario.

I was terrified of losing my relationships with the people in my life. Worst case scenario for me was that I would be completely alone. I would have nobody. And because of that, I would feel like I was unloveable. Once everything started into motion, and even as the divorce ended, I realized the people who truly matter in my life were still around. I was able to preserve what made sense for the relationships that were really important to me. I've even added some incredible people into my life because of the divorce.

SOMETHING NEW

Okay, listen, I never said I was perfect. At some point when I had nearly checked off my entire Divorce Bucket List—I say almost because "write a book about divorce to help others" was the last incomplete thing on my list—at some point, I may have re-downloaded a dating app or two; a girl gets lonely, okay?!

As I said, I had gotten through most of my list and had gone through a lot of growth. I did a lot of rebuilding and knew I didn't want to get into a dating situation where I would tear myself down again. So, I decided when going into this new attempt at dating that I was going to use visualization to create my perfect partner. I got out a piece of paper, and at the top, I wrote: "My Perfect Partner." I started writing; I began to think of the different things I had to have in a partner, knowing I had already been through a traumatically failed relationship that I didn't want to go through again.

I closed my eyes and envisioned what it would look like five or ten years from now to be sitting at home on a Sunday or traveling with that perfect partner. I pictured what it would look like to go on dates with that person, even eventually getting married again. What would it look like where I was at my happiest, whole, and fulfilled from the growth that I'd done since my divorce, not going backward at all? What did the person I could grow with look like, trait-wise?

My list did not involve any type of physical characteristics. It only had to do with qualities that I needed in a future partner and relationship. Once I wrote this list, I committed to myself that I was not going to settle for anything less than the things on this list. It wasn't some "Prince Charming" or something unattainable. It was a simple but defined list that was helpful because I was able to clearly characterize my goals for a partnership. Clarifying my expectations of a future partner ensured that I wouldn't let myself fall head over heels just to get rid of loneliness. If someone didn't meet these standards, I wasn't allowing myself to go down old roads.

I wasn't going to fall into the other dating traps that I'd succumbed to in the past. This time around, if I was going to do it, I was going to do it right, and I was going to do it in a way that would benefit my life and whoever I ended up with's life as well. I know that we don't live in a fairy tale world, and I wasn't trying to create a fairy tale. I was simply trying to set some realistic—not impossibly high—standards for the quality of relationship I wanted.

Once I made a list and the commitment to stick to it, I put the list away somewhere safe. Every once in a while, I would look at it just to continue to visualize it and make sure that my brain remained aware of what I was and was not looking for. I did not, however, obsess over the list. It was a side note to my life while I continued working on myself.

Little did I know that writing that list and making the commitment to myself would actually work. I found out, months later, when I stumbled upon the list again after starting to date someone quite amazing that this man met every single requirement! I hadn't physically pulled out that list as I began to get to know him; I only remained aware of it in the back of my mind. It was pretty neat to go back and realize, when I stumbled upon it, that the person I ended up dating was exactly the partner I was looking for and that my visualization did work.

I had set some standards for what I needed out of my next relationship based on things I had learned I did and didn't want through my self-discovery with my Divorce Bucket List.

This relationship I found became the healthiest relationship in my thirty-six years of life as of writing this book. That's not to say that all of my past relationships were bad, but I definitely was not at my best, nor were the people I was with at their best. Nobody's ever perfect, but it makes total sense why those relationships didn't work out.

As I write this, I am still with the man from the "My Perfect Partner" list, and things are going great. We've been together for a year and a half, and I could not be more thrilled to have found this man and have him in my life.

Whenever anyone asks us how we met, we jokingly make up different stories so that we don't have to tell them that we actually met on Tinder. But that's where it happened. I had decided when I re-downloaded the app that I wasn't going to play games. I was going to follow my intuition and give people a chance based on my gut feelings. I was going to open up my options and go in with the goal of meeting new people and no other expectations.

I'd probably been back on the app for about a week when I was headed out of town to Detroit for another speaking engagement. A couple of my business partners and I were taking a road trip from Pennsylvania to Detroit. I was sitting in the car in the passenger seat, legs up on the dashboard, when I got my first message from him. I thought he was so good-looking, and our conversation flowed easily.

I like to pick on him about this, so, of course, I have to include it in the book, but he didn't pursue me that heavily. Matter-of-fact, I had to resort to getting his attention from time to time in the beginning. It kind of drove me crazy yet was refreshing all at the same time, unlike the aggressive nature of many of the others I'd encountered on the app.

Things continued to bloom slowly, which is something that I wasn't used to. Everything in my life has always been fast and furious. With my new man, things have been progressing at a slower pace than I have ever allowed myself to go at, but it has turned out to be a much healthier and more rewarding experience.

As a reminder, my now ex-husband and I had a whirlwind of a romance. We had met in May, a week after his college graduation and only a year after mine. Everything was very passionate, quick, and exciting. We got engaged at the beginning of August, just three months after meeting. By that September, we were living together and finding out I was pregnant.

This new relationship, however, has been on a much healthier pace of exploration, which has allowed us to get to know whether or not we feel we are the partner who each of us is looking for. I'm not judging anyone based on the pace of their relationship; I know tons of people who got married quickly and are still living their happily ever after. And I'm so happy for them!

But that just wasn't my story.

Three weeks after my now boyfriend and I started talking, the COVID lockdown happened. At this point, we hadn't gone on a date or even met face to face yet. We had only talked on the phone once, yet there was a definite connection and an interest from both sides.

Throughout the pandemic lockdown in our state, we decided to continue pursuing things virtually. We started with video dates and really got to know each other. For me, video dates took "taking things slow" to the next level in this day and age. But it was so good for us. It helped us get to know each other and set a solid foundation for dating once we could finally get together in person.

Once the lockdown was lifted, we finally met for our first date, a walk in a park near my house. The pandemic was still in full force, so we didn't touch, we didn't even hug, let alone kiss, on this first date. Again, I was exploring unfamiliar grounds of baby-stepping into this relationship.

As we walked back to our cars and got ready to leave, he handed me a bag. Inside were a few packages of Cheez-its, one of my favorite snacks in the entire world, which I had mentioned in passing during one of our many video dates. Seriously, I will hike uphill in the snow, both ways, to get me some Cheez-its. Who knew it was that easy to win me over?

I came home from that date smiling ear to ear and called my best friend to tell her, "This is the one—he had me at Cheez-its!" To this day, he tells me he risked his life to get me those snacks because it was his first time going into a store since the pandemic had started.

Now, yes, we have our ups and downs. What relationship doesn't? But every up and down that we have is communicated effectively and worked through without resentment, grudges, or contempt. This man is so good to me, so great to my kids, and I'm so excited to see what the next chapter will bring with him. To think that all it took to find him was knowing what I really wanted and visualizing it!

Something Borrowed

One of the items on my Divorce Bucket List was to complete three home improvement projects. Leading up to the divorce, my ex-husband was typically responsible for most of the maintenance in the house. You know how it goes when you're married: you have these unspoken delegations of chores ... one of you does the trash, one of you does the dishes, one of you fixes the toilet when it's broken, one of you cleans up throw up when the kids get sick in the middle of the night—it's just this unspoken rule. It's crazy, though, because nobody ever really sits down and has this family meeting where chores are assigned to the husband and wife; it just kind of happens.

For us, when there was any type of maintenance around our house, it would typically fall on my ex-husband to complete. I decided that if I was going to be on my own, doing big girl things, I needed to do some of the things that I hadn't done around the house before. Three home improvement projects should cover it.

This experience is where something borrowed comes in because when my ex-husband moved out, he took almost all of our tools with him. That was fine with me because most were his. I guess it just didn't occur to me to replace these tools. So, a lot of these home improvement projects came with borrowing many different things from my neighbors. Thank you, guys, so much if you're ever reading this. I appreciate you more than you know for putting up with my nonsense.

I would text these neighbors and ask for random tools and objects to help with my home improvement projects. They've probably watched me from their windows, laughing at the blonde trying to install a Ring doorbell into a brick. That story is coming...

I also borrowed a lot of confidence to do these projects. I want you to know that even if you put something on your list to do or you're going to face some type of situation in your divorce that you don't feel equipped to handle, you can borrow the confidence to do it. Borrowing confidence is an okay thing to do; I borrow confidence all the time. It is a muscle that has to be built. You're not going to be confident until you do something over and over again because it is built off of competence.

When you believe you can do something, that's when you walk with the confidence to do it. So, if you've never done something before, you might not believe you can do it. It's only after you do it so many times that you start to accept that you're capable of doing that activity; therefore, you're going to have to sometimes borrow confidence to get started.

I borrow confidence by educating myself a little bit before doing something new or something I'm not confident in. I educate myself by reading, watching YouTube videos, or listening to podcasts. It's so simple to go into Google and search to find all kinds of resources for whatever you're trying to learn. For example, when I reinstalled a toilet seat, I had never done that before and had no clue how to do it—it turns out, it's supposed to be pretty simple—but I had no clue. I had to watch five different videos to learn how to do it. Then, when I encountered a few hiccups along the way—that story is also coming—I had to watch some more videos. I borrowed some confidence from the people in the videos who knew how to do it.

Another way you can borrow confidence is through affirmations. I'll get into affirmations more in the coming chapters, but they are seriously such powerful things! You can say something like, "I am a handyman" or "I am fearless." Whatever it is you're going to face, you can literally psych yourself up beforehand by telling yourself that it's already happened and you've already kicked ass doing it.

You can also borrow confidence from music. I can't tell you how often I've needed confidence that I turned on the loudest rock music I could find or some empowering songs to get my mind to an excited energy level.

Once I got myself psyched up to do these home improvement projects, I borrowed some tools and some confidence, and I got to it. The first thing I did was install a Ring doorbell on my front door, along with a Ring security system. Now, this might not sound like a complex project, and it probably shouldn't have been. I just need to throw in a disclaimer that while I may have a high level of intelligence and a couple of degrees, I do not have a lot of street smarts. This lack of street smarts translated into some of my home improvement project faux pas.

Anyway, back to the Ring doorbell. If you're not familiar with it, it is a video doorbell, which you can hook up to your Wi-Fi, phone, Alexa, etc. It will tell you when someone's at your front door, and you can see and speak to that person. I wanted this for security measures now that I was living alone. I was so excited to get it.

When I started installing it, I realized that the only place I could install it was made out of brick. The bracket to hold it requires screws to be drilled into the wall you're installing it on. Some of you reading this might have a better solution than what I came up with, but I ended up borrowing a drill, getting a long drill bit, and spending hours standing in front of my house, drilling into that brick. I was relentless and would not give up until I had holes big enough to fit the screws, put my bracket on, and finish this project.

I had neighbors approaching me left and right, offering advice, asking if I wanted their help. I refused to let anyone help me because this was my project. I needed to complete this to build that confidence because once I finished it, I knew I would feel more confident for the next one.

I'm sure that any other person in this world would have made this a much easier job, but hours later, I was so ecstatic when my Ring doorbell was finally set up! The holes were drilled, it was attached, I tested it out, and it worked. It was an incredible sense of accomplishment over something minimal, but it felt great.

I decided to replace a toilet seat for the next home improvement project because it had started to fall off the hinge.

Typically, this is supposed to be around a five-minute job and hardly any work at all. It's actually straightforward, but it turns out when you're me, things aren't always simple. So, again, I borrowed some confidence, and I said to myself, "You did the Ring doorbell; this is going to be a five-minute job. You've got this."

I decided to start installing the toilet seat around 2 p.m. I told my kids, "I'll be *right* back." I get to the bathroom and start to try and loosen the old toilet seat, only to find out that the nuts or bolts, whatever they are, were corroded completely to the toilet. If you're not sure what that means, it basically means they were so old that they'd essentially melted together. I could not remove them to remove the toilet seat.

I decided to borrow some confidence and pulled up videos of people who knew what they were doing. Then I texted two of my neighbors and asked them both if they had any power tools; specifically, I was looking for saws or torches. Literally, I was willing to try anything. I wanted to prove to myself that I could do this.

As it turned out, my neighbors had three different power tools they were willing to lend me. So, here I was, this clueless blonde, trying to fix a toilet seat with power tools. I spent the next five hours carefully using these power tools to hack away at the corroded metal and used a candle lighter to burn the stubborn pieces of plastic off of the corroded situation. Around 7 p.m., I finally posted a picture of my new toilet seat on social media with the following caption:

Today has been a journey... I spent a lotttttt of time fixing this toilet today ... it was a struggle, but I was listening to the lessons it was teaching me-sometimes life is shit (get it? Lol) but you gotta just buckle down and get through it no matter what is thrown at you ...there's always a path to a positive outcome even when it doesn't seem possible at times -sometimes you have to try a bunch of different things to find a solution ... it's not always what you think it's gonna be and if you give up at the first sign of failure instead of keeping on trying you won't get where you want to go!

I had taken five hours to do a five-minute job, but, damn, did it feel good to get it done. I didn't have to call someone and ask them to do it for me. I didn't have to rely on anyone but myself. I found that I was competent enough to figure it out, even if I had to borrow some things along the way. Do you know what that did? It made me feel so confident that I decided to take on project number three.

My third home improvement project was definitely not as exciting or funny as the other two, but it was something that needed to be done. Even though my ex-husband moved most of his things out when he left a few months prior, there was a lot of random stuff lying around from that chaotic, day-to-day life of a household. I decided it was time to clean out. So, I started going through the house, top to bottom, and getting rid of things; I did an embellished spring cleaning.

I started getting rid of things we didn't need by donating, recycling, trashing items, and just completely cleaning out the house. The hardest thing for me was when I cleaned out the office.

The office was just the third bedroom in our house, which we converted into an office. But for the last seven months of our marriage, it became my ex-husband's bedroom as we went through the separation phase before he moved out. That room was full of so many unknowns because he had left some stuff behind. It was full of bad memories of fighting, and it was the room where he had told me he wanted to get a divorce.

I had totally avoided that room for the first six months or so after he moved out, not even stepping in it once. I decided it was finally time to face it. I went to the room, and I started to slowly throw away anything we didn't need and clean it top to bottom to turn it back into the office it once was.

It was a very emotional day for me because I found a poem that my ex-husband had written about our journey that he had accidentally left behind in a drawer. It was so hard to read because it wasn't hateful at all. It wasn't an attack on me, but it was about two people who had met at such a young age and had children before they were ready, "children having children," I believe it said. He wrote about how that had created such a complicated environment and how we had become toxic and driven apart through it.

I knew that it would be difficult to clean out that room, but I did not realize that finding that poem would set me back emotionally for an entire week. It's okay to get setbacks. It happens. I want you to have that realistic expectation, so when it does happen, you can work through it and not beat yourself up about it. Once I got through that setback, I was able to move forward, improve my confidence, rebuild, and thrive.

Once I picked myself back up, I continued to clean out the room, to the point where I completely converted it back into an office and was able to work up there again. I had such an accomplished feeling when I was done. It was hard to get through, but I knew it was worth it once I had finished.

SOMETHING BLUE

When you're in a marriage, you have a partner. Even if that partner let you down in the past, or things seem to be breaking apart, you at least have that invisible security net of a partnership for as long as you're married. When you get divorced or are going through a divorce, you feel alone. Just because you're getting divorced doesn't mean the world's going to stop moving. Things are going to continue to happen around you. For me, some pretty crazy things happened, both in the world and in my personal life, as I was going through my divorce. The kind of things where you think, "Can it get any worse than this?" Things that cause you to look up at the sky and say, "Why are you testing me? How much further do you need to push me before I break?" Whenever I ask that the answer always seems to be: "As far as you need to be pushed until you recognize your own strength."

You will learn through these trying times that you can deal with traumatic events, again, on your own. You can be your own hero!

About six weeks after my husband moved out of the house, I decided to de-stress with a bubble bath one evening. As I had already mentioned, I had not consumed alcohol for a few months, leading up to him moving out. I knew that I tended to lean on alcohol when times were hard because of how I had depended on it while coping with my grandmother's death. Starting in December, four months before my husband moved out, I cut out all alcohol in order to keep a clear mind.

So, the story I'm about to tell you is even more interesting because if I had told you and not given you that context, you would have thought I was a bottle deep in wine. But two months after my husband moved out and six months after I stopped drinking for the divorce, I was taking a bath.

I had just put the kids to bed and decided I would practice some self-care and relax. I was sitting in my bathtub. It's one of those really deep bathtubs that you can actually soak in as an adult; one of the positive things that came out of having to remodel my bathroom after "the flood" that had happened. Anyway, I was sitting there drinking my favorite calming tea: Yogi Soothing Caramel Bedtime Tea—you can find it on Amazon; it's the best! There I was, sipping my nighttime tea, reading a book in the bathtub, just relaxing.

My youngest son knocked on the bathroom door and said, "Mommy, I'm scared. I can't sleep." A soldier committed to my mom duties, I got up and wrapped a towel around myself. I went into my boys' shared bedroom and tucked my son back into his bunk bed. I got him all settled, told him a story, and, once he was feeling better, I kissed him on the forehead. "Goodnight, buddy."

I headed back into the bathroom, ready to finally relax, when I noticed the water was cold. At that point, I didn't feel like running a new bath, so instead of getting back in the tub, I drained it. As I was starting to leave the bathroom, I noticed that my mug—one of my favorites—was still half-full of tea and perched on the rim of the bathtub.

I thought to myself, "I better move this," because I have this cat… a male cat, and oh my gosh, can he be destructive. My cat, Stitch, lives up to his name. He is so loveable and cuddly but also leaves a path of destruction wherever he goes; he simply cannot help it. He also loves the tub. He will jump in it with the water on. So, I knew if he saw a mug sitting there, he would knock it over and break it.

Still in my towel, I decided I should rescue the mug from its potential fate. I had rushed out of the bathroom to help my son and not noticed, but I must have dripped some water onto the tiles. I grabbed the coffee mug and started to leave the bathroom. As I did, I began to slip on the water on the bathroom floor. To catch myself, I lunged toward the marble countertop, mug still in hand. The mug came crashing down on the countertop, my hand still wrapped around it—as I said, the mug was my favorite mug, and I wasn't going to let it break. I was holding tightly to the mug to protect it and probably thought it would break my fall too. Well, it did; the mug broke my fall but also broke itself and sliced me right up the middle of my thumb, down to the bone.

I think I went into a little bit of shock at this point because typical me would have been screaming and crying, but I strangely felt zero pain. Had there been someone there to come to my rescue, I may have acted differently. What went through my mind at that moment was: "There's no one else here to be the hero but me. You have to be the hero right now, Jenn."

I immediately grabbed a towel and wrapped it around my thumb. The bone below the sliced skin still clearly visible. I realized that I had to get to the hospital, but it was 10 p.m., and I didn't have family in the area. There was no way I could drive. I ended up calling my ex-mother-in-law. She came over and took me to the ER. Thankfully, I had a sweetheart of a friend who was in the area by chance, and when I saw that she was online and asked if she could help watch the boys, she came over immediately and stayed with the kids. My poor kids had to help their indisposed mother get dressed to go to the hospital. They were so brave, my heroes!

I remember lying there on the floor and my kids just being so helpful. They were so brave and strong. At that moment, lying on the floor trying to keep calm and waiting for my ex-mother-in-law to arrive, I had another realization: if I could make it through this, we were going to be okay—my boys and me. I was going to be okay. I could make it through this. And I would make it through this divorce…I was going to make it through anything else that happened on the way through it.

As it turned out, I had sliced through the entire tendon in my thumb and required surgery. Surgery is up there on my list of top three fears with tornadoes and snakes. After returning from the ER, I found out I had to get surgery to repair and reconnect my tendon and that I'd never have full range use of my thumb again, which is on my dominant hand. I felt defeated but also realized I had to step up and become my own hero.

I went into that surgery headstrong and brave to show my kids and myself that I could do it. I came out okay, of course, and I spent the rest of the summer, including that Disney trip with my children, with a cast on my arm and hand—best summer ever. End sarcasm.

There are so many traumatic events that can happen to you while you're going through an already devastating period of your life, but sometimes I think divorce helps put those other crazy things in life into perspective. Once you get through something like divorce, you will feel like you can conquer almost anything. It might not feel like it if you just started, but I guarantee you that once you get through it, it will. Almost anything that's thrown your way, you'll begin to understand, is something you can conquer.

Another traumatic event that happened while we were going through our divorce was the pandemic outbreak of 2020. Because of COVID, our divorce, like many others at the time, actually took several years to finalize. The world, including courts, shut down. Lawyers became less attentive because they had to deal with the issues caused by the pandemic and lockdowns.

Everyone knows what happened with that pandemic; we all had our struggles, and I don't have to go into it in this book. For our divorce, everything got more complex because of it. Single parenting got harder, and we had to make changes in our custody schedule. We had to start communicating better despite our emotions. The kids had to adjust to a new way of life while still not fully adjusted to the new family dynamic from divorce; it was not easy. But we learned quickly that we could get through it.

We could adapt to the changes that are sure to continue coming our way as our kids continue growing, and that's the only thing we can do: adapt to these changes and grow and learn from them.

Exploration

For as long as I can remember, I've had a dream of traveling to London. For some unknown reason, I have been slightly obsessed with all things related to the Tudor dynasty and England. There's something about it that just speaks to my soul, and, to this day, I still cannot pinpoint it. Still, over the years, I've spent endless amounts of time reading and studying about Tudor history and England, London specifically, because of that.

One thing that has always been on my dream board is a trip to London. Every time our family vacation planning time would come around, I would pitch the idea of London, but it was just never a reality for us. It was super expensive and out of the budget for our family; it didn't make sense.

Life was busy with work, and it just hadn't happened.

As part of my Divorce Bucket List, I decided that I needed to do some type of solo trip for myself without knowing how, when, or where it would happen. I had this vision that I would rediscover myself through independence, fearlessness, and exploration if I went on a trip. I had no clue how I would afford a trip like that or let alone where I would go, but I understood it needed to be on my list: "Take a solo trip."

I knew going on some type of trip by myself would help me find the courage to rediscover that strong woman I once was. It would help me redefine who I was going to be after the divorce. This trip would help me find ways to be an individual again because traveling alone is no easy thing.

A few months into the divorce process, I was sitting at my youngest son's T-ball game. As I was sitting there, my phone started ringing, but it was an odd ring, not my standard ringtone. I noticed I was getting a video call from a corporate office. I was super excited to accept this video call because, usually, when this specific corporate office calls you, it's good news. I was optimistic that it would be something good, but I had no idea why they were calling.

Understanding the importance of the call, I stepped away from the sidelines of the T-ball game to take it. As I answered my phone, two of my favorite corporate partners were on the line. They asked me if I would be willing to speak to thousands of people at their upcoming, first-ever international convention. My. Mouth. Dropped. Wide. Open. I'd never been given an opportunity like this before!

Then, the unthinkable happened. I was informed that the conference I would be speaking at was taking place in London. I dropped to my knees right there in front of everyone. I knew people could see me, but I didn't care. I fell to my knees anyway and started crying into my hands as I gladly accepted the offer. I was being given the opportunity that I so desperately wanted and longed for. More importantly, I felt called to go on this trip so that I could share my story and help others—just like I was being asked to do! So, when I was given this opportunity of a lifetime, I accepted without hesitation.

I got off the phone that day completely honored even to be considered. Once my emotions settled, I reflected for a minute and realized this would be the solo trip that I had put on my list. When I wrote that I wanted to take a solo trip, I hadn't even imagined it would be my dream vacation. I only knew that I needed to take some sort of trip and that I needed to rediscover myself after previously spiraling.

I thought the solo trip I had added to my list would take years to plan and save money for. Like something out of a dream, it was now actually going to happen, and much sooner than I thought. It scared me because I wasn't sure I was ready. I was still working through the beginning of my list when this opportunity presented itself, so I was still stuck in the state of despair, depression, loneliness, being lost, anxiety, and I was unsure of who I was. How could I possibly travel alone? Was I ready?

With fear creeping through my soul, I thought long and hard for a few days. I realized that we're never really ready for anything. Even if I went on this dream solo trip and it didn't turn out to be the one that helped me find my independence, it would still be a step in the right direction. So, I looked at my budget and decided to find a way to get to London a week before the speaking engagement to explore and attempt to find myself again.

It turns out when you put your mind to something—even if it seems impossible—you can often find a way to make it happen. Maybe it was an early onset of that Must-Do Mindset? After chatting with a few people who were familiar with London, I found some deals and resources to book the trip. I ended up planning this trip four months in advance; the planning taking place much before I did many of the other list items that I shared with you. But the trip itself came after a lot of those items had been crossed off. I subconsciously forced myself to prepare for the big trip by doing the work, getting things done, and preparing myself for what I envisioned to be a finale of sorts.

Planning the trip also gave me something to look forward to while dealing with the negativity and emotions that often surround the divorce process. At the same time, I was so afraid because I had no clue what I was getting into or what would happen on the other side of that trip. At the end of the trip, I knew I would have my work obligations and feel fulfilled from those, but I had no idea if I would walk away from this trip feeling anything more than fulfilled on a work level. I hoped and longed and prayed that I would have received some form of healing and self-improvement when I got back from this trip.

As the trip got closer, my anxieties grew larger. I started wondering what I would do for an *entire week* in a foreign country by myself. I'd never been there. I didn't know my way around the city. I had no idea how to get around. I barely knew anyone there except for one or two distant acquaintances. And, to make it even crazier, I was going to be there on my birthday. Would I feel lonely being alone in a city far from my family and my children? Would this trip make me feel even worse than what I was feeling now? What if it all backfired in my face?

I was terrified of taking that long flight alone, especially having a panic disorder and knowing that, at any point, it could rear its ugly head again. I could be in a foreign country, having a panic attack, scared for my life. I did what I always do when I get anxious; I practiced my mind exercises, then I started researching and reading to put my mind at ease a little at a time.

I started looking into everything I could about the city and things to do while there, and I made plans for myself that I couldn't back out on. I committed to doing something every day while there, so I wouldn't sit in my hotel room in fear. I was going to get out. I was determined to make this the trip of my life; I was going to explore and finally see the city that I longed to visit for so long.

While I was nervous about flying alone, I had faith, from years and years of work on personal development, soul searching, and learning, that the universe always has your back if you open yourself to it. So, before I left, I asked the universe to give me a sign that I would be safe during this flight and protected during this trip, even though I would be a single female traveling alone in a foreign city.

That sign came a day after I asked for it. I had gone to get my hair done, and I found out that my hairstylist had a trip to London coming up as well. I was so excited for her and thought it was a neat coincidence. We got to talking a little bit further, and it turned out that she and her husband were on the same flight over as me. I can't explain it in words, but the sudden sense of calmness and serenity that came over my body told me that this was entirely destined to be.

I had put this trip on my list in a very vague description, and, somehow, it was being given to me because I needed it. It's so easy for us to get in our own way, and I almost did with my anxiety; I'm so glad I got the sign I did right when I needed it to move forward and actually go on the trip. I knew that it was up to me to get over my fears and put myself out there and just see what could happen.

The night before my trip, I was so excited that I couldn't sleep. I stayed up all night reading even more about the Tudor dynasty, London, and all its history. I read about current events, places locals go, things to do off the beaten path, and tips for female travelers. I read everything that I could think of to read about traveling in London. I even spent some time coming up with a hashtag for my trip: #JennSOLOndon.

When it was time to leave, I packed up all my stuff and headed for the airport. I sat at the terminal bar, got my ritualistic pre-flight IPA (for the nerves – I had allowed myself to have an occasional drink by the time of the trip now that I had my emotions more under control), and prepared myself for the journey of a lifetime.

The flight was long, but thank goodness for free wine, because I was able to fall asleep quickly on the way over.

I woke as we were landing. The butterflies were certainly acting up in my stomach, a bit of nervousness but mostly excitement. My hairstylist, her husband, and I met outside of the plane—a pleasant comfort—to get our luggage. We discussed possibly meeting back up for dinner one night, and I suddenly felt that no matter where I went in the world, whether I was married, divorced, single, widowed, separated, it didn't matter; I would not be alone. The truth is, we are never really alone; God/the Universe—whichever your belief—has our backs as long as we are open to it. Knowing that I had people in the city if I needed them was a vast comfort I hadn't planned on having, but the universe had delivered anyway. After retrieving our luggage, we parted ways, and I journeyed into the city alone.

I'll never forget my taxi ride from the airport to my hotel. It was about a forty-minute ride, and my driver was so kind. He saw how excited I was, so he took me on a private tour through different areas of London to get me acclimated. He didn't even charge me for the extra mileage, which I was wary of, being a single tourist and all. The driver was one of the friendliest people I had ever met; he told me so much about everything we passed. He pointed things out to me as we went, and I was full of more wonder than I had ever been in my life.

I had already fallen in love with the city, just within that short drive through it. I wasn't sure how it was possible, but somehow, I just felt an immediate connection. I like to call London my soul-city. I don't know if you've ever felt this emotion before, but being there evoked the same feeling I had when I held my children in my arms for the first time. I've also felt this emotion as I've witnessed others I've coached achieve something they worked hard for. It's a feeling that you are just meant to be right there, right then. There are moments in our lives when we just know we are exactly where we need to be, on our destined paths. This was one of those moments.

I arrived at my hotel, dropped my stuff off, and very quickly got ready because I had booked a bike tour around London for that afternoon. The Royal Bike Tour was a guided tour where we would take bicycles to see all the different royal landmarks in London. The excursion is something that I had booked online before I arrived. Online, it had mentioned that it would be a group of twenty. I wasn't that worried about a group excursion. It was still a little scary, but I was calm in the back of my mind because it was an organized event.

Once I dropped my bags off, it was time for me to take my first venture out into the city alone. Having no clue how to navigate my way around London, I simply looked at myself in the mirror and said, "If you can get through these past few months of your life, you can find your way from point A to point B in a city that you love." So, I did just that. I walked down the street from the hotel. It was a little scary at first, but I realized quickly that I felt safe there.

Lacking a few street smarts, I may have accidentally gotten onto the Tube without paying the first time because the system was a little confusing for this newbie. Don't worry; I corrected that for the rest of the times I rode, but it was a learning experience. It's something I can look back at now and giggle because it was such a different experience, and I can be a little oblivious at times. Thankfully, I didn't get in trouble at all, but the feeling of being able to figure something out that was extremely scary is so empowering, and that's exactly what I felt.

DIVORCE BUCKET LIST

As I finally arrived on the other side of London for my bicycle excursion, I was so thrilled to find that I was getting a private tour because nobody else had booked it for the same time as me. I couldn't have asked for anything neater in my life for my first day in London. The tour guide took me all around. He showed me Princess Diana's old home, her memorial, The Royal Gardens, Kensington Gardens, Buckingham Palace, Westminster Abbey, The Parliament, and so many other royal areas. He told me so many neat stories about the history of the city. It's weird because history was always my least favorite subject in school, but put me in front of Tudor or London-based history, and I'll listen in awe for hours.

We rode through so many different areas of London, and I got to see so many monuments and landmarks that I had only read about before. I think that's my favorite part of traveling: seeing or experiencing things in real life for the first time that you had previously only read about. It was like reading a book and then watching the movie afterward. When you read the book, you create the reality in your mind with your imagination, and then, when you watch the movie, you get to see it actually unfolding before your eyes. Sometimes the movie is not as good as the vision you created from reading the book, but sometimes the movie is far better than what you imagined in your mind. This city far surpassed my wildest imagination. By now, you know I'm a bit of a sap, so it's no surprise that my eyes were full of tears this entire bicycle ride. I couldn't believe I was there.

After my tour, I decided that it'd been a long day full of a lot of travel. I told my tour guide I was headed back to my hotel and which direction I was going on the Tube. I also asked him if he knew a local pub where I could stop to grab a quick pint on my way. He recommended I get off the Tube near Bank. Bank is a stop along the Tube near the Bank of England.

When I got off the Tube at Bank, I experienced my first moment of solo traveler panic since arriving in the city. I looked around, and I saw no pubs, no people. I only saw tall buildings and empty streets. I had no idea where I was, my phone reception was acting up, and the only choices I had were either turn around and get back on the Tube or go on an adventure. I decided I was going to try the adventure that night. After all, I hadn't come this far not to experience this wonderful city.

I walked a few blocks in the direction my body pulled me; I don't advise this, but I did it anyway. Shortly enough, I began to hear music. It was probably around 5 p.m.—happy hour! It was an abnormally beautiful day, as London's weather can typically be quite rainy and dreary. But this day was a beautiful 75 degrees with not a cloud in the sky. I walked toward the music and the sound of people—finally.

As I turned the corner, I saw the most beautiful sight. It was a very narrow cobblestone street lined with pubs—that's not the gorgeous part. The road was leading uphill, and at the very top was a break in all of the buildings through which you could catch a glance of St. Paul's Cathedral, the clear sky providing a breathtaking backdrop. It was stunning.

I began walking down the street and noticed that everyone was outside. I walked into the pub, and, aside from the bartenders, nobody else was indoors. It was like the bar had turned inside out, into the streets. That was fascinating to me because that's just not something I'm used to seeing in the U.S.

This view made me stop and think for a second. I realized that these people don't get to experience lovely weather like this on a routine basis, so the second they get it, they take full advantage of it—taking their happy hour beverages outside and not wasting a single second. As I reflected, I realized that I had been sitting around depressed and moping about the situation that I was going through in my life. Being so focused on despair, how much was going on around me that I was taking for granted? Had I been experiencing things that others would see as miracles, yet I was not living in the moment and valuing them? I made a conscious commitment to start being more like the people in the streets that day, focusing on the present and taking pleasure in the positives.

Over the years of working on myself throughout my divorce, I had learned that when you focus on the good, you see even more of it in the world. So, how dare I let somebody else's reflection of me and an experience in a traumatic event, such as divorce, take all of that power to enjoy the good away from me.

I made a decision right there, at that moment, with St. Paul's Cathedral hovering at the top of the street within view, that there was not going to be another day that I didn't find something great in it. I decided that I would live in a moment of wonder every day. It could be the beautiful weather that day, a hug from my child, or the fact that my kids were getting along. It could be a work accomplishment, or it could be the fact that I have a roof over my head and food to eat. From now on, I would be committed to honoring this scene that I witnessed, and I would appreciate the little things more consciously. That's when I started my gratitude journaling.

Deciding to be more actively present and grateful in the moment, I ventured back to the beautiful Kensington Gardens the following day. It was there that I made my first gratitude journal entry:

I am sitting here in the beautiful Kensington Gardens in London. It's another gorgeous, sunny day, and the sun's warmth can be comfortably felt through the shade of the trees around me. The sound of the five surrounding water fountains gently flowing into a beautiful pond provides a sense of tranquility. I'm surrounded by relaxed families, couples, groups of friends, and even some who appear to be fellow solo travelers. I feel at peace in this moment, witnessing the miracles of life all around me. There is so much beauty in the present. I am thankful for this serenity, this beautiful day, and these views.

That trip went on to be the most amazing trip I've ever been on, even though I went alone. I made so many memories in London that I could write another book dedicated entirely to that trip. I got to tour many historical places, stand in spots where world-altering events took place, experience a day at boozy brunch with locals, and my birthday the following day at an inflatable adult obstacle course with new friends. I partied the night away with people I'd never see again. I ate the most delicious meals in historical settings. I danced with and kissed a tall, dark, handsome Italian man. I drank pints with my dinner each night and lived out things I'd only previously dreamed of. I met people from all over the world and learned so much.

More importantly, I began the steps of exploration I needed to find myself again. It wasn't until the end of the trip that the most magical thing happened, but, first, we must look at some of the other things I had been doing behind the scenes along the way and leading up to the trip!

Doing The Things

I included many things on my Divorce Bucket List that were not necessarily "story" worthy for this book; however, they are essential in the healing and rebuilding process, so I wanted to share them with you in the form of some tips and tricks.

Empowering Activities

Throughout my journey in completing the items on my list, I found some things to truly empower myself to feel more confident in getting through the experience. Here are some areas I suggest you explore to find some things to add to your own list:

Join a New Hobby or Group – Doing this is really bene-ficial for a couple of reasons: First, when we start going through a divorce or separation, the support system we envision being there is not always what it seems to be. So, not only will finding a new hobby or group build your skills and confidence, but it will also help you build your support system. The analogy I like to use is going to a buffet and using one of those flimsy Styrofoam plates. With the plate in hand, you start going down the buffet line and put some pizza, roast beef, mashed potatoes with tons of gravy, corn, and fries on it. If you do this, your Styrofoam plate is just going to collapse from the weight. When we are going through a divorce or separation, it is one of the most traumatic things you can go through. Therefore, it is very easy to overwhelm and exhaust our support system, just like that Styrofoam plate at the buffet line. However, you want all that good food—just like you need a lot of support. So, if you go up and put a little bit on one plate, go back to your table, and then go put a little more on another plate, and repeat the process until you get all of your food—none of those plates are going to break. They're all going to be there to support your food—aka you. Then you're going to be able to enjoy all the food—aka rebuild, regrow, and get through your situation with a great support system! Finding a new hobby or group is an excellent way to spread out your Styrofoam plates while also finding self-confidence!

Reconnecting – This could be reconnecting with anything that brings you joy. Often, when we are in a serious relationship or marriage, we become consumed in that relationship and disconnect from other things in our lives. I want you to think about things like friends, family, coworkers, and hobbies that used to bring you joy that maybe you lost touch with, but you can now reconnect with.

Rediscovering – Again, it is easy to get lost in marriage and relationships because you are no longer just yourself; you are part of a unit. Once that unit is no longer in place, you have to reconnect with yourself to truly flourish again. I love to rediscover myself through journaling. Journaling allows you to really start connecting with yourself again. It's also easy to succumb to negative thinking and self-talk as you're going through divorce, separation, something that's traumatic, breaking down your confidence, or heightening your fears. Even if you journal once a week, what you're doing is positively reconnecting to your thought process. There are some great examples for journaling prompts later in this book.

Setting New Goals – This is going to help you rebuild your confidence. When you connect this with journaling, you're going to start building your confidence, rebuilding your life, and thriving. As cliché as it may be, I again picture the butterfly that goes from being this kind of ugly caterpillar thing to a beautiful wonder. The caterpillar has to get really messy in that cocoon before it emerges (literally, it breaks down into a gooey mess), but it comes out as a beautiful butterfly when it does arise. You can do that, too. Just like the cocoon, a divorce is very messy. However, a messy and traumatic situation doesn't mean you can't come out on the other side, being the most beautiful version of yourself. By starting to set new goals for yourself, you're able to do that. Selecting your goals and working towards them is like getting your hands messy in that cocoon. I used my Divorce Bucket List approach to identify my goals and start taking baby steps towards those goals to rebuild and thrive completely.

Gratitude and Affirmations – I love practicing gratitude and affirmations in my day-to-day routine. Gratitude is thankfulness, and affirmations are things you can say that you want to exist in the future, except you phrase them like they are happening right now. Starting with gratitude: to implement that into my life every night before I go to bed, I either write down or think to myself what I was most grateful for that day. It could be anything from

"I'm grateful for my coffee today" to "I'm grateful for my health" to "I'm grateful to be alive." When it comes to affirmations, I do those in the morning, and they can be anything from "I am worthy of love" to "I am a good person" to "I am in a happy relationship again." It just depends on what you desire and what you need to reinforce in your brain. You tell yourself these affirmations every day, and you're going to start rewiring your brain into a positive place. Saying these affirmations also helps you visualize what you want so that you can more consciously work towards it. I could go on for hours and hours and days and days into why this works, but I'm going to need you just trust me on this one.

Let's dive deeper into some of these empowering activities in the following sections.

Visualization For Healing

I want to teach you about a piece of what I've done to make these enormous transformations from helpless and terrified during a divorce to ultimately thriving through and after it was done. I'm about to share a piece of the practices that I implemented into my life and that I work with my clients on in order to start thriving through the divorce/separation experience.

The one piece that I'm talking about here is visualization.

I'm going to get a little nerdy on you: Our brains control what we pay attention to. We go through our daily lives, processing millions of pieces of information. We only pay attention to—or absorb—certain pieces of information because our brains literally filter things through. That filter basically uses your active thoughts to tell you, "Oh, you're interested in this, pay attention!" or "Oh, that doesn't seem important to you, ignore it."

The journey through a rough experience, such as a bad marriage or the trauma of a divorce, can rewire our brains in a way that causes us to live below our desires and true potential. Therefore, we have to take control and rewire our brains. We rewire our brain by growing new neurons and strengthening the connection between our existing neurons. There are types of wiring that exist in our brain that connect things through experiences, memories, and thoughts that tell us what to focus on and pay attention to in our lives.

You get to look at life in one of two ways. You can look at it as either it's happening to you, or it's happening around you while you get to react. When you look at it as it's happening around you and you choose how to react and perceive it, then you're going to live in a much better place and truly thrive.

Now that we know that the wiring in our brain is built and strengthened by thoughts and experiences, it still takes some practice to really view life as happening around you, with you having control over the perceived reality you are experiencing. Consequently, we have to strengthen those bonds in our brain to look at the things in our life that way. Now, it does get a little bit more complicated than that, but I think the basics are all we need before I show you what I and many others are doing to help us during the divorce/separation experience.

Think of the wiring in your brain as a type of muscle or bond—the more you do something, the more you're strengthening that bond. Every time you practice these exercises that I give you, you're going to be wrapping a layer around a figurative wire that's just going to create more strength in the bond—or muscle. In comparison, if you have a piece of toilet paper, you could very effortlessly pull it apart; it's not a very strong bond. But if you take some toilet paper and start wrapping duct tape around it and then another layer of duct tape and then another layer, it's eventually so strong it can't be pulled apart by hand at all. That's how you create rewiring in your brain to go from traumatic experiences to completely rewired and thriving. I've read stories that many successful professional athletes use visualization similar to the techniques I'm about to teach you to improve their performance on the field!

Here are two of my favorite things that are simple and easy enough to start doing right now to use visualization to rewire your brain:

Affirmations

The first thing you can start doing right now to rewire your brain and begin thriving through your divorce or separation is practicing affirmations every single day. Affirmations are a way to rewire your brain by training it to think differently. It's very, very easy when we go through divorce or separation, or even a traumatic experience in our life, to start thinking negatively and start the whole "woe is me," and life is happening to me thinking. It becomes scary; there's so much fear, right?

Affirmations are something you will want to incorporate into your daily routine, either morning or night, so set yourself an alarm for when you might have a free minute to repeat a few sentences to yourself! Do them every single day with your alarm until they become a habit for you. When it's time to do your affirmations, you could just read them, you can say them out loud, you can dance while you sing them aloud—it's entirely up to you and your comfort level.

I've learned that everything around you changes when you start doing this and making a habit of it. You start to fully believe the affirmation and pay attention to the opportunities that appear in your life that allow you to make these affirmations come true. Because you are saying these statements out loud, that brain filter I mentioned earlier will start paying attention to the things in your life that will serve those statements and filter them into your brain more efficiently. The filter will work with the affirmation statements to reinforce and build the thoughts into reality. It's not magic; it's brain science! You're doing those exercises much like if you want to get abs … you can't do one stomach crunch one day and then thirty days later look down at your shining six-pack! You have to go out there, and you have to keep doing those exercises over and over until your stomach forms into the washboard you desire. The same goes for practicing affirmations. I want to give you an example of what those affirmations might look like.

Here are some of my favorite affirmations that you can tell yourself to help as you are going through a divorce:

- I am a good person with a lot to offer.

- My heart is healing.
- I am confident and strong and improving my life every day.
- I can handle this.
- I have an opportunity now to create the life I want.

All of these are so true, whether you believe them yet or not. I guarantee that when you start implementing affirmations into your daily practices, you're going to begin not only believing it but seeing it, too.

Journaling for Visualization

Another one of my favorite things that you can start doing right now is journaling. You don't have to be a writer; you don't have to write pages upon pages. You can just fill in the blank, or you can even just think of your answers and not write anything down. The point here is that when you start reconnecting and rediscovering yourself, you're going to start empowering and rebuilding those confidence blocks you need to truly step into a thriving mode.

You really can't get anywhere until you start rediscovering who you are, what you need, and what you desire.

Here are some examples for journaling prompts:

- My perfect life a year from now would look like this:
- Lessons I learned from my most recent relationship are:
- If I could have the perfect day, it would be:
- You could write a letter to yourself dated for a year from now about how proud you are of where you think you will be. (This is creating another visualization of who you're going to be so that you can start working toward being that person.)
- Currently, my greatest fears and worries are:

HEALING THROUGH REGIMEN

In addition to using visualization, I started implementing a pretty simple routine into my life. When I started going through my divorce, I found myself hitting rock bottom. I was at the lowest point in my life. I didn't know who I was anymore and was completely terrified. I was hopeless. I realized things needed to change if I wanted to stop existing in survival mode and use my experience to create the life I wanted, so I started implementing a couple of practices into my daily routine. Here is what it looked like:

Implemented the "5 Second Rule" – This is something I learned from the outstanding Mel Robbins; she has a book called *The 5 Second Rule*; I highly recommend you read it.[1] This practice helps us overcome fears and objections that happen in our brains. You simply have a thought, countdown from five, and take action;

you're refocusing your brain from overthinking the situation and talking yourself out of it to "five, four, three, two, one—go!" This practice is something that I specifically implemented in my morning; I love to start my day off with the 5 Second Rule when my alarm goes off. I do not hit the snooze button. Instead, I have trained my brain to say "five, four, three, two, one—stand up!" Just like Mel Robbins taught me, I keep my phone on the other side of the room, so I have to stand up to get to it. Doing this makes me get up and get my day moving, and it starts my brain off in the right place because I'm not going back to sleep and disrupting my natural sleep patterns.

Morning Affirmations – I already went over these in great detail earlier, but it is essential to incorporate them into a routine so that they become a habit. The only way they work is if you do them!

Immediate Hydration (Water) – I cannot get enough water into my body. I know this sounds silly, and you are probably thinking, "How's water going to help me through my divorce?" When you fuel your body correctly, you're going to feel so much more positive and ready to tackle your day and any challenges that come with it.

Small Wins – I try to get a small win quickly in the morning. A quick win can be something as simple as a skincare routine or making your bed. Just have something on your to-do list every day that is an accomplishment for you that you can quickly check off. This approach is all about boosting your confidence levels. Once you raise that confidence level and feel like you've accomplished something, there is research out there that shows you are more likely to get even more done.[2] Quick, small wins help you with your productivity as well as your confidence.

Evening Gratitude – I usually practice my gratitude at the end of the day, as I'm lying down to fall asleep at night. I write down what I experienced that day that I'm most thankful for in a journal—or you can just tell yourself in your head. It allows me to reflect positively on the day and train my brain to focus on the positive, no matter how good or bad that day went. As a reminder, life is either happening to you, or it's happening around you, and you're controlling your perception of it. I want to help you guys realize that your divorce is not happening to you. Instead, it is a gift and an opportunity that you can use to reframe your life where you can rebuild, regrow, and truly thrive.

Your daily routine does not have to look exactly like mine. It could incorporate some or all of the things above or different things you have learned from other places that will positively impact your mind, body, and soul. The important thing here is that you start doing something every single day to improve yourself to begin to rebuild and reach your desired outcomes.

THE CROWN

Divorce can be quite a journey. It can be heartbreaking, exhausting, traumatic, and scary. It can also be beautiful, freeing, and a true adventure toward your desires. I already mentioned how fear can get the best of us and be quite an interesting beast to conquer, but I hope that reading this story has helped you feel empowered and a bit more courageous to go after your desires and thrive through and after your divorce.

Wherever you are in your journey, you may be finding yourself apprehensive and afraid of all the unknowns to come. You may feel unstable like the entire ground has fallen out from under your feet, or you may feel like you can't see what the future holds. It is totally acceptable to feel that way; let those feelings go through your body, but then take some time to think logically and start battling the fears so you can prosper and define your new chapters in life. The anxiety and fright that you may be feeling in your situation are very normal, but by completing your own Divorce Bucket List, you could turn that anxiety and fear into excitement and hope!

We often fear that upcoming situations will be scarier than they are. Think about it: when was the last time you were afraid of something before experiencing it? Before that event, how bad was the fear, in your mind, on a scale of one to ten? Once you experienced the actual event, was the experience as bad as what you were expecting? Did the worst-case scenario you had worked up in your head actually happen? Was it as terrifying as what you were expecting? My guess is it was not nearly as high on the scale as you had worked it up to be in your mind—yes, there are exceptions. In general, we tend to talk ourselves into over-exaggerated fear because our minds were built to protect us.

My son's reaction to his shots at his ten-year-old wellness visit is a perfect example of this over-exaggeration of fear in the mind versus the outcome of the actual event being feared.

It was time for my oldest son's ten-year-old well visit, in which he was required to get some vaccinations, and he knew about this going into the appointment. I want to reinforce that he was not three or five years old in this story. He was ten years old and had gotten many shots before without any issues at all.

Leading up to the appointment, my son was highly anxious. He kept asking me if he was going to have to get a shot. "Mom, please, I don't want to get a shot," he repeated over and over on the way to the doctor's office. I reassured him that he had shots before, that they had not hurt him then, and that he would be fine. He said, "I know, but I'm just so scared because I don't remember how it feels, and I'm afraid it's going to hurt."

No matter how much I reassured him that in the past he was okay, he had still created this fear in his head that the shot would be the worst thing that he would ever endure. These conversations continued all the way up to the appointment. I did my best to calm him down and let him know he would be okay.

We got through the appointment fine, but I could see that he was shaking, nervous, and a little on edge. When the doctor said, "All right, you're looking good, buddy. I'm going to go get the nurse," my son knew that it was time. He immediately started freaking out. He started—and I cannot make this up—running around the room in circles screaming and flailing his arms above his head. You would have thought a live T-Rex was chasing him.

Tears were streaming down his face, which was red from panic, and he kept screaming. "No, I don't want to, I don't want to. Don't do this to me. It's going to hurt. I can't do this." He was screaming all of these things about how afraid he was, yet the nurse hadn't even entered the room yet.

Once the nurse entered the room, she realized that she was going to need some backup. We tried to calm him down just enough for her to administer the vaccine; however, anytime he started to breathe normally, he ended up working himself back up into a state of frenzy.

The nurse decided to call for backup, so we had three nurses, plus me, in the room, and we were going half an hour into this event. I could see the expression of fatigue on the nurses' faces. As a last-ditch effort, they asked me to help them restrain him—one of the hardest things to do as a mom is restraining your child when they are terrified. But I assisted the nurses in holding him down while I held his hand.

Finally, after about five more minutes of wrestling with him—the strength of a frightened ten-year-old is unheard of—we restrained him well enough so that they could administer the shots.

His shirt was soaked in tears, and he was visibly shaking. The nurse counted down from three and gave him his shot. Within an exact split second—there was no wind down from the frenzy—my son's face just went completely blank and calm. He looked up at me and then had the actual audacity to smile and say, "That didn't hurt at all." I've never cringed so hard in my life.

We laugh about it now, but it is very representative of the fear that happens in our brain all the time. The fear that we have most often is based on non-situational fear; it's not something that's actually threatening us. It's the thought of something that could be or might be. My son was afraid that he might have extreme, excruciating pain. The pain never happened for him. Instead, he suffered through over half an hour of panic and fear, leading up to an event that, in the end, never hurt him. Divorce is a lot like that. Throughout the different stages of divorce, you'll find yourself completely scared of the change and the unknown, of what's to come, only to discover that as you go through it, everything ends up not being as bad as you expected it to be.

Some studies show that intentional change can be the scariest type of change to encounter. We are so fearful of change because change brings with it uncertainty. Neuroscience research has shown that our brains register uncertainty like a computer would register an error.[1] When we face uncertainty, we go on high alert, thinking something is drastically wrong. In reality, we are simply just facing change and the need to adapt.

There are different types of fears. There are physically present fears based on exposure to events that could potentially be threatening—for example, seeing a snake. Then there are non-physically present fears with no immediate cause—nothing is immediately happening to cause harm, for example, the fear of the unknown. A lot of the fear we encounter around divorce has to do with the second of these examples, and the good news is that most times, when the dread you are feeling is non-physically present, you end up realizing the outcome wasn't as bad as you thought it would be.

When you start battling with fears that are holding you back from reaching your desires, I encourage you to grab a piece of paper and journal—or answer in your mind—the following regarding that fear:

- What am I afraid of, specifically?
- What is the worst-case scenario outcome of this fear happening?
- What can I do to prevent that worst-case scenario (or maybe ask someone else to help me do)?
- If the worst-case scenario were to happen, how can I get back on track afterward?

By completing these prompts, you will find that the fear you are facing may be less scary than you initially thought. You may discover that if the worst-case scenario does happen, it won't be as bad as you originally thought. This exercise is the exact questioning I did to assess the worst-case scenario for attending the wedding alone, among many other things throughout my journey. This exercise has helped me calm my brain through fear to get back to completing the items on my Divorce Bucket List to truly thrive again.

This brings us to the rest of this story...

You know, it's crazy. You start going through a divorce, and you feel like your life is over. In reality, you're looking at an opportunity to either sink into despair or have the freedom to truly reach everything you've ever desired—to truly rebuild and grow to the person you want to be and achieve the things you want to achieve. I had no idea how much my relationship with my former spouse held me back from achieving the things I wanted in life. Now that I look at it in hindsight, that is not a relationship I desire.

Everyone deserves to be with a person that helps them advance, grow, and build. I'm not saying you have to be number one at everything; I'm just saying you find these experiences to grow and just become better than you were a week ago, a month ago, or a year ago, and you do it together. The relationship I was in was so toxic. And it was actually pulling me backward.

I had not realized this when I was in it because it's hard to see things from an outside perspective when you're in something.

Think about it. Let's say you're getting a group picture taken. The photographer can see the whole picture. However, from inside the group, your perspective is different. You can only see the photographer and anything in your direct line of vision. Once the photo is taken and you're looking at it from the outside, you can notice much more about it. You can see who was smiling, laughing, making a silly face, touching, and what was really going on in the situation. When you're in it, you don't have that full perspective.

So, it wasn't until I got out of my relationship that I was able to see how much it was holding me back. Once this realization set in, I became grateful for the journey I was on because I then knew I had this new power to start doing the things that would help me advance, build, grow, and flourish in life again.

I was so ecstatic when I got that phone call at my son's T-ball game to speak on stage in London. It had been my dream to be an international speaker, and it was happening. Somebody saw the potential in me. It's interesting because that had been my dream for most of my marriage, but it didn't happen until after the divorce papers were filed. It was that little nudge that I needed to realize that sometimes you have to give up something that you're comfortable with to get something even better in its place.

Throughout the experience of my Divorce Bucket List, I had a lot of breakthroughs. As I completed each task from my list, I learned a new lesson about myself or divorce. I felt more empowered, and I felt more confident with each item I completed. But the one that brought everything home for me was the trip to London. Traveling alone in a different country, speaking on that stage, I felt at home. It had been so long since I experienced that feeling, and, honestly, I don't even think I felt that at all through my entire marriage. It gave me so much hope.

The day before my speaking engagement, one of the business partners I was working with had arrived in London a day early. We decided to go to Buckingham Palace because it was open for tours when we were there, which doesn't happen all year long.

We decided to go for a tour of the palace. When you tour the palace, you find yourself in a couple of long lines waiting to get in. It was in those lines that my friend and I started having some conversations. We started talking about symbolism since she had been going through some struggles in her life as well. It was almost like the world had brought us together at that very moment, on purpose, because we both had the exact same idea.

When she asked me how the trip had gone, because I had been there for almost a week before she arrived, I told her how amazingly life-changing it had been for me. I told her that I felt like I finally put the crown back on my head. And she said to me, "that's crazy because I literally had been considering getting a crown tattoo while I'm here in London!"

I gasped, pulled up the photo gallery on my phone, and showed her the ideas for my crown tattoo, which I had been saving to my phone since I had arrived in London. We had the same idea!

We proceeded through the tour of Buckingham Palace, and, oh my gosh, if you ever get the chance to do it, please do it. It has so much history that it gave me chills. The palace is gorgeous. It's amazing. There were downtimes during the tour, where we were waiting to get into a new room. During those downtimes, we were on Pinterest and Google looking for different crown tattoos and trying to pick one out because we decided that we were going to get it done after the tour.

Not only was I figuratively going to put the crown on my head while I was on this trip, but I was also literally putting a crown on my forearm. We kept looking at these crown tattoo ideas and were just not falling in love with any of them and starting to feel discouraged.

We walked through these beautiful gardens and came across the palace's ice cream shop as we were leaving. The shop had this gorgeous, strong, yet dainty crown on the top of the building.

I looked at my friend, and I said, "That! That's the one!" We took a picture of it and decided we wanted just a little bit of liquid courage first. We headed to a pub around the corner, which, yum, there are still days where I crave a pint and some fish and chips from London—you wouldn't believe it but with mashed peas! Don't judge me ... they're delicious!

So, we get our pints, eat our food, and search for tattoo shops in the area. We finally found one with excellent ratings. By this time, I had already learned how to navigate the city confidently. It felt empowering to have this feeling of direction, like I belonged in this city. I've never felt like that anywhere else in my life.

This experience was my first time getting a tattoo in another country, so I was a little apprehensive as we walked into the shop. Part of me was hoping it was appointment only.

It was not.

Here's a big surprise—when my tattoo was finished, I took one look at it and immediately was in tears. These were tears of joy, freedom, bravery, and pure enlightenment. Being big on symbolism, that was such a transformational moment for me.

After that, I went to a corporate party where they rented out Tower Bridge for us. I don't know if you've ever seen pictures of Tower Bridge, but it is gorgeous. It was nighttime, and we got to ride on a cruise down the Thames to get there.

As I mentioned, I have a bit of an obsession with the Tudor dynasty. So, the Tower of London and all of the surrounding areas were places that I had explored a little bit on my own already, but I had not gone up in Tower Bridge. I'm so glad I got to experience it. Being in the lit-up Tower Bridge at night and then inside at a private event was one of the neatest moments of my life. It is something I will never forget.

When I walked in, there were two long corridors. They were completely lit up and gorgeous. Appetizers were flowing. I had business relationships with a lot of the people there, so I felt like I was surrounded by people who were on the same path as me. They were working to grow and advance and be better in life, too. It was another one of those "I'm meant to be here" moments.

Having shown up directly from getting my tattoo, I had fresh ink, so naturally, everyone asked me about it. I got to tell them my story about how I had gone from the lowest point in my life where I didn't even think it was possible to continue forward to finally feeling like I was on the path I was being called to. I explained how I finally felt like there was so much hope and like I finally loved life again. I realized as I was telling the story that I had finally fallen back in love with myself. My colleagues all said that I had to tell that story in my upcoming speech because they knew so many people would need to hear it. I knew, too, that I had to tell my story one day, like I am now, to more than just the people who would be in that room.

The next day, speech day, my voice decided that it didn't exist. I suppose this happened from all of the excitement and touring. Do you guys remember the part where the whole reason I was there in London was to tell my story to inspire thousands of people? Well, now I didn't have a voice. I was panicked, and that's an understatement. I am so grateful for the people I was surrounded by at this event because they came to my rescue.

If you've never been part of a group that lifts you up on your way to where you want to be, I encourage you to get out there and start looking for that group. It is the best feeling in the world to find people who encourage you to do the things that you love. One of my favorite things about my current relationship is that my partner supports me. In fact, as I was writing this book, I canceled our date night one night to meet a deadline. Not only did he understand, but he showed up at my house with dinner because he knew how overwhelmed I was. Then he gave me ideas and helped me brainstorm. He, beyond doubt, just supports everything about this journey.

In my marriage, whenever I was working on something to better myself, I was guilt-tripped. For example, when I was working on getting my MBA, I was ridiculed for any time I took away from him or for causing him to take on more responsibility with the children due to my classes. When I decided to start pursuing my career goals and dreams, I was mocked. As I was receiving training in the living room, he would walk by and mimic what they were saying and the personal development that I was doing to try to have a better mindset. He would mock everything so much that it beat me down and made me think my desires were either silly or not possible.

I digress; let's bring it back to London, my dreams to help others about to happen. I was about to get on this stage, and I didn't have a voice. It was so ironic that I had the most I'd ever wanted to say in my life but without the voice to do so.

My speaking engagement was scheduled for late afternoon. All morning, I kept drinking tea and using lozenges, and not using my voice at all. I was doing all the things everyone was telling me to do. We were trying to get my voice back. It was so important to get this message out to others. You can't go on stage and speak if nothing comes out when you open your mouth.

There were moments where I felt panicked, like: How am I going to be given an opportunity I've always dreamed of and then have it taken away from me? Am I going to have to cancel?

I don't know what was responsible for what happened next. But amazingly, less than thirty minutes before I was supposed to go on, my voice came back; it was like someone or something knew that people needed to hear what I was going to say, and I was being given the ability to say it. I'll never forget the relief I felt.

As I figuratively put the crown on my head on that stage, finishing the speech, I received a standing ovation. My dreams had come true. And it wasn't about me. I wanted to inspire and help others, and I was able to do that; knowing that I could do that was so fulfilling. I was able to turn this experience that was absolutely traumatic and devastating, that some people hardly make it through, into something that could help other people. And forever, ever, ever, I'm going to be grateful for that.

I feel that gratitude every day of my life, and I am now living what I call my happy not-ending. I found happiness and ways to cope when things didn't go my way. I feel like I'm living my true purpose.

Don't forget to take some time to appreciate the journey as you go through your divorce or separation. If you're having one of the most challenging days or are experiencing conflict that you think you can't get through, then take a step back and look at it and say, "I am so grateful for this part of my journey, because I'm going to learn something from it." I want you to look at your entire journey, be grateful for all of it, and know that you can learn something from every single thing you experience through this journey. You are going to come through stronger, and you are going to be even better. You're going to rebuild. You're going to flourish. You're going to thrive.

Don't forget to appreciate the moments. Look at things outside of the moment as you go through it, so that when you are at the point where you feel on top of the world when everything has finally recovered, you've rebuilt again, and you're happy, you will have those memories to know how you got to where you are. You will put your own crown back on as you fall in love with yourself and life again, and maybe, just maybe, you can even help one other person do the same by showing them it can be done.

I want to leave you, the reader—and now my friend—with what I said at the end of that speech in London in hopes that it touches you. No matter where you are in your divorce or separation journey, I want you to know that you are not alone, there is hope, and you can truly thrive in your wildest dreams on the other side. You might be only considering a divorce, you might be in the middle of a messy one, your divorce might be finalized—and you're ready to move on, or anywhere in between. Wherever your journey currently is, the rest of your book is up to you. It's up to you to take action, and when you use the tools that I've given you and implement your own Divorce Bucket List, I know you will be able to find joy and peace as I, and many others, have.

The day I finally put my crown on and gave that speech, it wasn't just for the people in that room; some of the words I spoke that day are for you too:

When I was asked to come to speak to you guys, I was just starting everything with the divorce process. I told you guys that the beginnings of the divorce broke me, right? I had spent years prior to my divorce doing all kinds of self-improvement that had built me up. I felt amazing about myself because of the work I had done. Then this divorce crumbled that work to the ground again, and I found myself building from scratch. I was not okay.

I found myself in a place where there were days that it was almost impossible to find the strength and energy to get out of bed, let alone work on my goals. I spent so much time in a state of despair and self-pity until I almost lost everything, including my own life, my sense of worth, and my true identity. I finally said to myself, "You need to find yourself again; you need to find your worth again. Because until you do, you're not going to be able to fill other people's cups, and you're not going to be able to live the life you desire."

Deciding that I needed to do something BIG to make some changes, I came here to London a week early, before this event, for a solo trip. I got here, and it was kind of scary trying to navigate everything by myself, something I'd never done before. I've never ever traveled outside of the U.S. by myself before. Yet, after the first day here alone doing the scary thing, I felt accomplished.

What happened by the last day of my solo adventure… I fell in love—twice!

You guys are probably in shock, thinking I shouldn't be tampering with love when I'm still not officially divorced. But this is the kind of love that I needed and was searching for.

I fell in love this week, once with the city of London, because it truly is magical.

And second, with myself, as I rediscovered who I am, what I deserve, and what I am capable of.

As you are working towards your dreams and goals, I want you to make it a point to do something out of your comfort zone and do it soon. That doesn't mean be as dramatic as I was and go to a foreign city by yourself; I simply want you all to do something out of your comfort zone that will help you find yourself a little more. Something that's going to help you discover yourself and fall in love with yourself, despite all the things you've been put through. Do something that is going to challenge you just a little, so you know what you are capable of.

After all the things that I've been put through - bullying, death of a sibling at a young age, my parents' motorcycle accident (where they almost lost their lives too), eating disorders, a toxic marriage, a challenging divorce, battles with panic, anxiety, and depression, and so much more...I realized that I went through those things because somebody listening to this needed me to go through them so I could stand here and tell you all that you can get through what you are going through and also achieve your dreams. And so, for that, I'm grateful for my challenges.

When I fell back in love with myself a few days ago, I decided to honor the transformation with a tattoo of a crown, symbolic of the one I finally put back on my head after all of the struggles I had been through; finally finding myself and worth again.

I want you guys to all do something with me before I leave you today. I want you to hold out your hands (yes-literally do it right now) – Imagine you are holding a crown, the most beautiful one you have ever seen, full of royalty and power. Now, raise your arms, with your invisible crown still in your hands, and put that crown on top of your head. Carry that crown with you for the rest of your life because you deserve all of the amazing things coming your way.

~ **The End**

You can learn more about working with Jenn here: divideguide.com.

DIVORCE BUCKET LIST

JENNIFER HARRIS

Notes

The End

Weir, Peter. 1998. The Truman Show. United States: Paramount Pictures.

It's a Marathon

Brad Kane and Lea Salonga, "A Whole New World," Walt Disney, 1992.

Doing The Things

Mel Robbins, *The 5 Second Rule: Transform Your Life, Work, and Confidence with Everyday Courage* (Savio Republic, 2017).

"Completing this task first thing in the morning takes seconds—and it can make you more productive all day," CNBC, March 2019, https://www.cnbc.com/2019/03/18/making-your-bed-first-thing-can-make-you-more-productive-all-day.html.

The Crown

"Science Says This Is Why You Fear Change (and What to Do About It)," Inc., November 2017, https://www.inc.com/scott-mautz/science-says-this-is-why-you-fear-change-and-what-to-do-about-it.html.

Acknowledgments

Grateful doesn't even begin to cover how I feel towards a vast number of people, without whom this book would not have come to be. I truly envision this book changing the world by helping inspire others to thrive through their divorces, creating a ripple effect of sharing their post-divorce success stories to encourage even more people to overcome and thrive too.

It's so hard to remember every single person that I want to acknowledge—writing this section is more challenging than the book itself, haha. If you had any part in my divorce journey or providing encouragement or feedback on my ideas for this book, I am wrapping you up in a collectively colossal THANK YOU!

Thank you to my parents and brother for being the true definition of family and putting up with me for all of these years. Your support of my activities and dreams has never gone unnoticed, and I thank you for being present and encouraging me to dream big. Without that encouragement, I would not be the dreamer I am today, and this book wouldn't exist.

I want to thank all of my family for supporting this endeavor, especially my Nanny and Pappy – you both support me in so many ways, even if Pap can be a brat—just kidding!

I am also highly grateful for the memory of Grandma and Pappy Gus—their love and support early in my life helped me become who I am today.

To my boys, Colton and Camden: I can't even express how blessed I am to be your Mom. You have taught me so much about life, and I am so proud of both of you for the incredible men you are growing up to be. Thank you for letting Mommy take the time to write when she needed to and for cheering me on as I completed this book. I will always return the enthusiasm as you both reach for your goals in life.

Tim, you are my person. You believe in me more than I believe in myself, and your encouragement not only as I was still going through the divorce process but also as I was writing this book is something I will be forever thankful for. I love you!

To all of my friends that stuck it out while I battled some pretty heavy shit...I love you, I appreciate you, and I am here for you in return. Your grace in acceptance has allowed me to overcome many things I needed to get through and make this book a reality. Thank you for sticking it out, helping me brainstorm, and providing feedback and ideas as I went through the writing process.

For those that helped with the development and production of this book itself, I could not have done it without you, and I am forever grateful that you helped me turn this project into a reality:

-To my editors Jessica Gang and Kaitlin Travis, who made excellent suggestions along the way and really polished my work into something that is enjoyable to read, thank you.

- To the team at GetCovers, thank you so much for the breathtaking cover design. It is so symbolic of my journey from the pool to the crown. Your creativity, communication, and finished work exceeded expectations.

- To everyone else who worked behind the scenes, including my formatter Walt, your expertise is beyond appreciated.

- Ann Ritts, I never thought I would say this but thank you for suggesting we run the half marathon. That race became a huge part of my Divorce Bucket List adventure and contributed significantly to my healing.

- Ali Ersheid, you always had such great insight to contribute as we discussed the development of this book over the past two-plus years; thank you for encouraging me to keep my voice strong. And thank you for all of the mentorship you provided throughout my divorce; it was invaluable.

- Erica Roberston, my partner in crime! As I wrote this book, I realized that divorce is what brought us together. While it sucks that we both had to endure what we did, I am beyond grateful that you are in my life! Thank you for all of the venting sessions and unconditional love as I got first through the experience of divorce and then while writing this book. P.s. I know your last name is changing soon… I guess I'll have to update this then; so, so happy for you!

Lastly, but certainly not least, to all of the individuals I have had the opportunity to coach through their divorce journey… Thank you; you have inspired me more than you will ever know.

JENNIFER HARRIS

Work With Jenn

For More Resources or To Work with Jenn:

Divideguide.com

DivorceBucketList.com

Facebook.com/DivideGuideJenn

Instagram: @DivideGuideJenn

To inquire about booking Jennifer Harris for a speaking engagement, please contact the booking team here: hello@divideguide.com.

JENNIFER HARRIS

About The Author

Jennifer Harris is an author, speaker, divorce coach, and the creator of the Divorce Bucket List coaching program. After experiencing her own traumatic marriage and divorce, she went on to become a highly trained and certified Confidence & Transformation Divorce Coach. With over ten years of coaching experience, she's passionate about sharing her story of the grief and trauma she experienced and how she developed the Divorce Bucket List to help her move forward. Jennifer is dedicated to inspiring others to achieve their desired outcomes through divorce and rebuild their lives to emerge from their separations into happier, healthier chapters of their lives. She currently resides in Pennsylvania with her two wonderful boys.

www.ingramcontent.com/pod-product-compliance
Lightning Source LLC
Chambersburg PA
CBHW030907080526
44589CB00010B/184